MAGIC IN THE MUG

DISCOVER A LIFE OF PURPOSE IN A SINGLE CUP OF COFFEE

BRANDON HAIR

Magic in the Mug: Discover a Life of Purpose in a Single Cup of Coffee

©2023 The Story Collective Co., LLC
www.magicinthemug.com

Cover & Interior Design by One Eleven Creative
Photography by Amber Clark Photography

979-8-9884784-2-3 (Paperback)
979-8-9884784-1-6 (Hardcover)
979-8-9884784-4-7 (eBook)
979-8-9884784-3-0 (Audio Book)

ENDORSEMENTS

Magic in the Mug is a captivating journey that uncovers some profound wisdom hidden within the world of coffee, from its humble seed to the comforting warmth of a mug. As a coffee enthusiast, I was amazed by how Brandon connected the art of brewing with life's greatest purpose. This book not only satisfies the palate but also nourishes the soul, offering insightful leadership lessons that resonate long after the last sip.

—RYAN FRANK
CEO/Publisher at *KidzMatter*

I don't know about you. But I myself am a wholehearted coffee lover! Even as I write these words, there is a delicious cup of coffee right next to me. But I must admit that Brandon Hair's exceptional new book, *Magic In The Mug*, makes me look at coffee in a whole new way.

Brandon takes us all on an unforgettable journey to unlock our purpose and deepest fulfillment. And as the philosopher once said, "When we have a big enough WHY, we can withstand any WHAT." Overlook this book at your own peril.

—DR. JEANNE MAYO
Public communicator, Author, & Coach
President & Founder: The Cadre Mentoring Experience, Platinum Leadership Coaching, Prevail Women's Mastermind

I love coffee and I also enjoy it when my life feels purposeful. A book about both of those things? Yes, please. Brandon writes in a way that gets to the point but with humor and the wisdom that only comes from lived experiences. And a whole lot of coffee. Coffee and purpose: two great tastes that go great together. Ok, I suppose one isn't actually a taste. You get it though.

—JACK HOEY III
Pastor, Speaker, Editor of this book and many others

Indulge in the captivating parallels between the world of coffee and life's profound journey in Brandon Hair's *Magic in the Mug*. As a coffee lover, I was captivated by Brandon's analogy that mirrors our path of refinement, from the moment of salvation to the fulfillment of our destiny. With every sip, his words resonated deeply with my personal journey: "Just as coffee beans undergo transformation, so do we." Through relatable anecdotes and spiritual insights, Brandon guides us from the initial stages of growth to the joyous culmination. *Magic in the Mug* is a rich brew of inspiration, reminding us that, like coffee, our lives are crafted with patience, faith, and an unwavering commitment to step into our purpose.

—SHANNON D. HAIR
Author, Speaker, and Founder, SimplyFreedom, LLC

Brandon's book takes you on an interesting journey from coffee seed to mug. He relates this to life's challenges when trying to discover your unique, God-given purpose. Brandon provides practical advice and scriptural references mixed with a great sense of humor and personal stories that you will enjoy. Oh, and after reading this book, you will have a different level of respect for that mug of coffee that you sip each morning.

—DAVID MIKE
Author of *Dishonor: One Soldier's Journey from Desertion to Redemption*

Magic in the Mug is a clever, powerful allegory, written with an honest, witty voice—true to its author, Brandon Hair, and his own journey. There's a poignant message for readers in their own journeys too. Brandon, and thus his writing, is relatable, likable, and engaging; his story, Christ's story, and the reader's story are all revealed in these pages, and this teacher couldn't be prouder!

—HOPE MURPHY
Brandon's High School English teacher, Author of encouraging notes, Host of parent/teacher conferences, Director of Children's Ministries

TO MY WIFE, MY FAMILY, AND TO EVERYONE ELSE WHO HAS
CO-AUTHORED THIS STORY THAT IS MY LIFE. THANK YOU
FOR THE PAGES WHICH BEAR YOUR FINGERPRINTS.

CONTENTS

FOREWORD

So much can happen over a good cup of coffee. You pour a cup at home or place an order at your favorite cafe and, in doing so, create space for a purposeful conversation.

It might just seem like a moment with a cup of coffee, but is it?

No matter how you take your coffee or where you choose to drink it, those moments can be holy moments if we allow them to be.

The phrase, "Let's get a cup of coffee," universally indicates that a time of connection is coming. Sometimes, that time is used more transactionally, like for a business meeting or a conversation with a friend. However, sometimes those seemingly insignificant yet purposeful moments spent sipping alone and connecting with the Father can be the catalyst to open our hearts and minds to experience God's presence and His purpose for our lives.

God speaks to us through paused moments and as we tune our spiritual ears to hear His voice. Removing distractions as we read the Bible and slowing our lives down, even the length of time it takes to enjoy a cup of coffee, can help us shift our perspective and gain the clarity we need. Here in His presence is where we hear His voice, sense His love for us, and ultimately find the purposeful paths He has for us.

Have you ever noticed there's something about church people and coffee? The two just go hand in hand. And since the church where I serve is just a stone's throw away from the local Starbucks, well, needless to say, I have been known to be there a good bit. As a fellow coffee lover, my frequent visits to the coffee shop have not only fueled my mornings but have given me a location to read, study, have a meeting, or refuel for the second half of my day. Over those cups of coffee, God has shaped an awareness of His presence in my everyday life that led me to write.

I wrote the very first piece I ever published over a cup of coffee in the corner of my local Starbucks. In my book, *Waiting On Wonders*, in the chapter called "Missing The Storm," I recall how I was confused, trying to sort through complex emotions and working to process my swirling thoughts that particular day. As I read my Bible and sipped my coffee, I became consumed with what I was reading—so much so that the rest of the world seemed to disappear. My *problems* didn't disappear, but the more I read, God spoke to me about my situation through the stories, characters, and passages, and my next steps became clearer. In the corner booth, over that cup of coffee in His presence, I could sense a path forward, and it was at that moment I knew that the Lord was doing something special in my life. He was weaving together what I learned in that paused moment and revealing my purpose.

The actual cup of coffee didn't change my life. However, had I not stopped long enough to enjoy that cup-of-conversation with the Lord and His Word in that coffee shop that day, I would have missed out on something He wanted to cultivate in me. And, come to find out, it had been brewing under the surface of my heart for many years. It just needed time to grow in the soil of patience, steep in the heat of intentionality, and be brought to the table of my heart at just the right time so I could taste and see the Lord's good plans for me.

Have you ever felt that you were searching for your purpose? Have you been cruising through life but not sure about what you're doing or even how to do it? The Bible is full of people who felt the same way and how the Lord opened their eyes to the "more" they could become.

Brandon Hair and *Magic in the Mug* offer a glimpse into their stories. I have had the pleasure of knowing Brandon and his family for many years. Our paths initially crossed in ministry and then, over time, at Starbucks as my barista. In *Magic In The Mug*, Brandon takes us on an agricultural and spiritual journey to teach us about our God-given purpose. From farm to cup, he weaves practical biblical lessons and stories into the painstaking process of growing, harvesting, and bringing that beloved liquid motivation to your cup. As he does, he teaches us more about who we are and how to live this awesome life that God has for us. It's a beautiful reminder that all creation points attention to the Lord daily and reveals His nature and character to us. (Romans 1:20).

So, with your favorite magical coffee drink in hand, enjoy these pages as you, with paused intentionality, listen for the voice of the Lord speaking to you.

There is magic in your mug - and it is God's love calling you to your divine purpose. May you enjoy every sip.

—TARA BANKS
Worship Pastor and Author,
Waiting On Wonders, 40-Days of Wonder Devotional

PREFACE

"MAGIC BEANS ARE REAL. THEY'RE CALLED COFFEE."
— SOME RANDOM INSTAGRAM POST

The hardest part of my day used to be the time between waking up and when I finally heard my percolator finish brewing. No longer. As of Christmas last year, I have a coffee maker with a timer function. Now, my coffee is ready for me the second I wake up. And while I absolutely love this new set-it-and-forget-it situation I've got going for me, there is also something to be said about working for that first fresh, hot, morning brew. The old way was nearly a guarantee that, as long as beans were in the cabinet, I would start my day with a successful endeavor.

Automatic timer or not, one of my favorite parts of the day is still when I take that first sip. I won't call it the best part of my day because that would be extremely shallow (I do have a family, after all) and would mean that my day can only go downhill from there. But it is without question one of the regular highlights. Here's a little secret though: It's not really about the coffee, it's about what it represents. It's a brand-new moment, a brand-new day, and a brand-new opportunity to experience life and love, joy and pain, relationships and community. At that moment, everything seems right with the world, and I am in a place where I can appreciate a new opportunity to walk with the Lord in everything He has for me. I should remind myself of all these things way more often than I do, but that's what the coffee is for.

As you can probably infer, coffee is one of my first thoughts when I wake up in the morning and when I get hit by that massive truck known as the afternoon lull. More than a simple pick me up or cure for the exhaustion that seems to plague humanity, coffee has a lot to teach us if we will take the time to listen. Learning and experiencing the coffee process has been a huge part of my life and has taught me some valuable lessons. It has illustrated some deep and formative truths in ways that you can literally taste. In the pages ahead, we'll explore that journey together, have a few laughs at the expense of my younger self, and hopefully learn some ways that you can move closer to becoming who you were created to be. Can learning about coffee really help me discover my purpose? Yes. Remember, it is magic.

I remember when I had the idea for this book. I was in a pretty dark place and trying to figure out who I was, why I was here, and what I had to offer the world. I wish I could tell you I was some twenty-year-old on a backpacking trip through Europe during a gap year where I was hoping to find myself, but I wasn't. I was in my mid-thirties and had just lost my job in ministry. Every thought that came into my head during that time told me it was time to pack it up, to move on, to relegate myself to busy work that would just pay the bills. By that point in my life, I had done many jobs in and out of ministry and despite some great seasons, I could never seem to find the right fit. I didn't fit in the construction world, I didn't fit in the business world, I didn't fit in food and bev or retail, and now it seemed I didn't fit in ministry either. Honestly, I thought I'd never find my place.

One day while sitting in a coffee shop, I took out a pen and started making two lists. Where was the joy and where was the fruit? That's Christian speak for "When was I happy and when was I effective?" That list began a journey that got me back on track. Finally, I can say I am living a life filled with purpose and passion. It's not always perfect and there are still really hard days, but I know who I am, who I am becoming, and why I am here.

I have come to realize that my journey was not unlike the journey coffee takes to get from a seed to the cup. The process is filled with dark times, pain, tension, and challenge. There are also times of rest and times of waiting. Times when the progress is quick and visibly obvious, and times when the progress takes a bit more patience and can't be easily measured. Despite these ups and downs, on the other side of the journey, we find something beautiful, something worth waiting for, and something worth those beans going through the fire and giving their life for.

I hope you'll take that journey with me and maybe begin your own process. It will be difficult at times, and it may not be as quick as you would like, but it will be worth it in the end. You too can find something beautiful that is worth the wait and even worth committing your life to. So, brew up a cup of the good stuff, take a sip, and let's experience the magic in the mug.

INTRODUCTION

For we are God's handiwork, created in Christ Jesus to do
good works, which God prepared in advance for us to do...
—Ephesians 2:10 (NIV)

In the pages that follow, we're going to go on a journey. It is a journey that extends through time, covers great distances, and is steeped in history, legend, and mystery. It is a journey in which we will combine three of my favorite things: talking about Jesus, telling stories, and, of course, drinking coffee. The journey that coffee takes to get from the seed to the cup is one that can teach us a lot about our own journey and purpose. Honestly, when you put Jesus, stories, and coffee together, it's amazing what you can discover and accomplish.

I began to fall in love with coffee shortly after becoming a youth pastor in 2007. It was a habit born completely out of necessity. I was newly married and just beginning my ministry career. Shortly thereafter, my wife and I would have our first child. Needless to say, I had a few demands on my time and sleep fell farther and farther down the priority list. As a result of this sleep deprivation, my undiscovered desire for coffee found a secret metaphorical jet pack and rode it all the way until it sat, triumphant, at the top of my regular thought process. The more I learned about coffee and what was possible, the more I began to like it. The more I liked it, the more I drank it. The more I drank it, the more trouble I got into with my new wife for spending all of our money on coffee; a habit that she admittedly, just didn't understand. I quickly realized I would have to find a new way to "support the habit." Because of how often I was there, I began to build relationships with the baristas and truly appreciate the team culture at my local Starbucks. They all seemed to be reasonably happy and well-adjusted people, so I thought, "Why not kill two birds with the same bean?" (See what I did there?)

I applied for a job and after all but stalking the manager of the store, I finally convinced her to hire me instead of taking out a restraining order. This job would provide my wife and me with an additional income stream and allow me to decrease my coffee spending without all the nasty side effects of cutting back on my newfound obsession. The more I learned about coffee and the company, the more I loved it. I used to believe that magic happened behind an espresso bar. Once I learned how to use one, I realized that my hypothesis was absolutely true. There was something magical about that place. That magic was found in the people and the stories that were collected and shared over a perfect cup. There's just something about a good cup of coffee that brings down walls and allows people to connect.

KNOWLEDGE AND THEORY CAN NEVER COMPETE WITH A TRULY IMPACTFUL HANDS-ON EXPERIENCE.

While working there I gained valuable experience in the obvious areas such as customer service and crafting delicious beverages. At the same time, I was also gaining knowledge in the process of growing, processing, and roasting high-quality coffee. While all of it was interesting, it was a bit of a challenge for me to memorize and wrap my head around the ideas that I was not able to practice. I could read documents and watch videos about processing and roasting all day long but at the end of that day, I never actually did any of it. Thus, my passion for coffee's "pre-retail" journey stagnated while my love for the final product continued to grow. Through all of this, I learned that knowledge and theory can never compete with a truly impactful hands-on experience.

A few years later it would all come full circle when I finally had an opportunity to experience those parts of the process I was missing. My wife and I took a trip to Hawaii with her family to meet up with my sister-in-law for a much-needed vacation. She lived in Sydney, Australia at the time so Hawaii was actually the halfway point. Tough situation, right? In the weeks leading up to the trip, my wife and I sat down to discuss what we wanted to do while we were there because apparently sitting on the beach and staring at the ocean with our mouths hanging wide open wasn't quite enough. We talked to our travel agent, did a few web searches, and were instantly inundated with a seemingly limitless number of options. Despite the wide variety of possibilities, I made but one request for our time on the islands: I wanted to visit a coffee farm.

Hawaii is one of only two places in the U.S. that have quality coffee farms. Since I didn't plan on visiting Puerto Rico anytime soon, this trip would provide my best chance to fulfill that request. We started doing research on farms and the types of tours they offered. We finally decided to go to Kona and visit a farm where I would get to roast and package my own coffee from beans grown and processed right there on the farm. Afterward, we would get to take all 5 pounds of high-grade 100% Kona coffee home with us. Being that close to the process finally allowed me to experience the parts of the journey I had been missing. I realized there is something magical in every step of the process, not just in the shops. The growing, the processing, the roasting, it all has an impact on what that bean will be like once it is in the cup. With coffee, everything matters. Every step, every process, and every minute detail factor into the final flavor. These details are what make coffee so unique and alluring.

The lore surrounding coffee's origin is an incredible story that starts over 1200 years ago. Like any epic tale, it is riddled with heroes, villains, romance, and treachery. It is a story that starts with a goat herder and his hyperactive livestock and eventually comes to rest on your table in a delicious cup of your favorite roast with the perfect amount of cream and sugar. It's easy to take that cup for granted; to forget how far each bean had to travel to get from a tiny seed to your cup. It's easy to forget what that seed went through to transform from its tiny origin into that massive tree and eventually through the arduous processes and painful experiences to become something more than drinkable; but something magical.

For most of us, coffee is part of our daily routine. It has become a staple to people all over the world. In fact, 3 out of 5 people say they "need" a cup of coffee to get going in the morning. After all, there's nothing like taking that first sip while sitting in your favorite chair with a good book before the rest of the house wakes up. Some even go so far as to say that they don't drink coffee for themselves, but for the sake of everyone around them. Coffee is the second most traded commodity in the world trailing only oil and Americans alone drink more than 450 million cups a day. Needless to say, coffee is kind of a big deal.

For some, it's love at first sip. But it is a testament to the power of coffee that millions of others have acquired an otherwise lacking taste, simply because of what coffee does for them. Whether it is the mom of four kids under 10 years old, the pre-med student getting ready for that dreaded senior year final, the writer stuck in between a hard deadline and a very real case of writer's block, or the police officer getting called to a crime scene 20 minutes before getting off of third shift – for all of them and so many more, coffee isn't just a drink; it is a necessity. We've come to embrace the power of this tiny bean when we are struggling, but most of us don't realize what we can learn from the struggle involved in making coffee itself. If we look back at how it got from its farm to our cup, examine each step of the process, and apply its lessons to our lives we can become a bit more purposeful, passionate, and, dare I say, flavorful as people.

Coffee must be planted, grown, harvested, processed, roasted, packaged, shipped, ground, and brewed before we can drink it. The time it takes to get to the cup is in extreme excess of the time it takes to consume. Our lives are the same. An athlete spends much more time practicing than playing in games. A musician practices more than she performs. For every painting an artist sells are thousands of sketches lying around their house. Everything we do, everything we face, and everything we achieve can be part of our greater purpose if we just take the time to pay attention to the process and learn the lessons we're presented with.

But be warned, unlike coffee, our process is not always linear. My own process has been anything but. That's why in the following pages you'll see stories from a year ago as well as stories from my childhood. We may talk about my teenage years and then jump back to adulthood. That's ok, we're people, not plants. Our lives aren't about getting from point a to point z, it's about learning and growing and becoming the best we can be while embracing our own journey.

I hope that what happens throughout the following pages is exactly that. I hope you find yourself in a place where you can discover your purpose and chase your dreams. I hope that by sharing some of the Truth from God's Word and the lessons I've learned from my own stories, you will find the energy and tools you need to become all that you were created to be. As you read these pages, beware, it is easy to attach a sense of purpose to a label, a job title, a business, or a follower count. I want to encourage you to make sure you don't miss the point. As you seek your purpose, take life and the lessons as they come. Every experience you walk through is about taking a next step toward that ultimate purpose.

*A VERY IMPORTANT DISCLAIMER

Finally, at the risk of burying the lede, our purpose is not actually about us. It's all about how God has created and designed us. It's about how we interact with and follow Jesus and how we encourage others to do the same. We have a choice to make: We can live a life characterized by striving to accomplish and struggling to check boxes, or we can live a life characterized by His love, His glory, and His peace. We can live our lives trying to point to ourselves and grow our personal kingdoms or we can live lives that point to Jesus and seek to advance His kingdom, the only true kingdom. The truth is, without Jesus, without the life that He provides, and without the purpose that He injects into that life, it's all meaningless. None of the rest matters. It's all about Him and when we submit to Him as Lord, that's where we find true purpose, true joy, and true freedom.

As we prepare to embark on this journey, let's be reminded of the fact that Jesus took a much more difficult journey on our behalf. Like coffee, Jesus went through a process that starts with planting. He came to live among us, planted in the midst of His own creation. He saw people, recognized their value, and called them into kingdom work reaping a harvest that would cross generations and centuries to find its way to us. He went through the process of fusing His deity and humanity into one. Becoming a God-man who could walk with His own two feet upon His world and allow His creation to relate to and walk with Him. He endured suffering and pain, betrayal, and mockery that must have felt like walking through a fire until He was nearly consumed. Finally, He went to the cross, killed in a fashion reserved for the worst of criminals despite His innocence. His flesh was ripped apart and torn as if to grind Him down to nothing all so that we could be made new. Through all of this, His life was poured out as a sacrifice so that we could have full and lasting life. This isn't a simple morning pick me up, this is true life. This is new life, abundant life, and a life that counts and matters because our Creator says so. Do you have that new life? Do you have the life that Jesus offers? Do you know Him?

If you do, I pray that the pages that follow will allow you to fall more in love with Him and to take hold of the abundant life that only He can offer. If not, I pray that you will take another look at Jesus. Study His life, His teachings, and His sacrifices. Know that He lived His life with you in mind and that He is waiting with open arms for you to come home. Find a pastor, a mentor, or a friend and explore Jesus together. Scripture reminds us that if you seek Him, He will find you!

I will admit that it is possible to be what the world considers successful, accomplished, and even happy without Jesus. But it is impossible to find true purpose, to have a truly eternal impact, or to experience real and authentic joy without Him at the center of it all. I pray that you find your way to this kind of relationship with Jesus. He is better than anything this world has to offer you. And it is He who can truly give you a life of purpose. Without Him, this is just a book about coffee. Which, you know, is wonderful, but it's still just a drink. Now, let's dive in and follow coffee along its journey from seed to first sip and discuss all of the challenges and struggles that those magical beans endure as they get to a point where they can be the pick-me-up we need each morning and, in the process, let's discover our own magic in the mug.

CHAPTER ONE

SO, YOU BOUGHT A COFFEE FARM

"IF I HAD AN HOUR TO CHOP DOWN A TREE, I WOULD SPEND THE FIRST FORTY-FIVE MINUTES SHARPENING THE AXE."

—ABRAHAM LINCOLN

Ok, so you probably didn't actually buy a coffee farm. If you did in fact buy the farm and subsequently bought this book to learn how to turn that farm from a vast expanse of undeveloped nothingness into a densely populated grove of trees that produce the gloriously caffeinated nectar on which so many have come to depend daily, then I apologize. This is not such a book. However, if you hang in there with me you may learn a few things about yourself, your life, and your purpose anyway. The first of these things is that research is a necessary first step in any new business venture. I mean seriously, who buys a coffee farm before doing a little research? What if I told you that a single cup of coffee could point you toward your dreams and your purpose? Maybe this premise sounds a bit far-fetched but stick with me. You don't need to buy a whole coffee farm; there's magic in the mug.

The magic in the mug comes from its journey. From start to finish, coffee goes through transformations and changes that make the final product extremely different from its origin. The coffee journey covers thousands of miles, countless hours, and intense processes. And it all starts with a plot of land that its owners hope will become a lush and active farm someday. I imagine staring at that plot of land and being completely overwhelmed. I imagine there are quite a few things on that untamed and unprepared plot of land that could stand in the way of the farmer's goals. There would likely be vines, rocks, hard soil, animals, and even stringent governmental regulations that could potentially stop any new crop from growing.

When it comes to coffee everything matters and you have to get it all just right. The location of the farm is just as critical as how you tend it. Coffee only grows in very specific conditions, conditions which are only found within the climates of the earth's equatorial zone. That zone is located between the Tropics of Cancer and Capricorn and is why there are so few coffee farms in the United States. The only US states or territories located in this zone are Hawaii and Puerto Rico. One of the critical conditions found in this zone is altitude. Coffee typically only grows above 1500 feet. To grow the really good stuff, your farm probably needs to sit above 3,000 feet. Hawaii is a bit of an exception because of its nutrient rich volcanic soil. So, if you have a volcano, bonus points to you. High altitude matters because these climates have ample moisture in the air. While that makes it sound possible to grow coffee in Colorado, it isn't. Beside the fact that my skin has never been less hydrated than when I lived in Denver, it's also way too cold. Coffee thrives in temperate environments making the right combination of temperature and altitude critical. There are plenty of places around the world that have one, but not the other.

In addition to temperature and altitude, coffee thrives in regions that have distinct wet and dry seasons. The wet seasons are ideal for planting and growing while the dry seasons provide the perfect opportunity to harvest and prepare the beans for the long journey ahead. Trying to find the right balance of these factors while also adding the right balance of sunlight, the appropriate amount of water, perfect drainage, and a superb soil containing exactly the nutrients needed, makes growing coffee as easy as trying to get an eight-year-old to eat their dinner. If you are unfamiliar with this concept trust me when I say it's difficult. Their "needs" are a moving target. Their favorite food last week is offensive today. In coffee cultivation and juvenile nutrition, conditions must be perfect and even still, there are no guarantees.

All of these obstacles must be addressed and removed before the real work can begin. Before our hypothetical farmer friend can begin the work of planting, harvesting, or processing, they must start by preparing the land. Once any hindrances have been removed (and proper government forms filed, of course) they must then cultivate an environment that encourages and supports growth. This practice is not a one-time thing. Fields must constantly be refined, cultivated, and renewed in order to continue to produce fruit. New weeds will sprout and new wildlife will move in threatening to choke out or consume the new growth. But the committed farmer is always willing to put in the hard work necessary to keep his fields in a position to support new growth and sustained life.

Living our purpose and chasing our dreams is a lot like this. Before we can begin chasing these things, we must prepare our hearts, our minds, and our lives. We must prepare our hearts for the inevitable ups and downs that happen along the way. We must prepare our minds so that we can have the focus and tenacity to stick with it when it gets hard. And we must prepare our lives so that we have the space in our schedules and on our calendars to dream big dreams and pursue our goals. This part must include the people close to us. Living your purpose and chasing your dreams without the support of your spouse, family, and close friends is like trying to grow coffee in Detroit. One of the necessary conditions for our growth is community. We aren't designed to, and we shouldn't, do this alone.

THERE WILL BE SOME GOOD, OR EVEN GREAT, THINGS THAT HAVE TO BE REMOVED FROM YOUR LIFE IF YOU WANT TO MAKE ROOM TO SAY YES TO AND PURSUE THE BEST THINGS.

So, the conditions are right, you've prepared, and you have support. There is something else we need to address: Distractions. The fact is, there are a lot of good or even great things that you can do that are outside of the purpose for which you were created. These things, while fun and exciting, become nothing more than distractions if they keep you from pursuing your purpose. They can act as weeds and rocks in your path to cut off, choke out, or even completely kill your dreams. Don't get stuck living a distracted life. Be relentless in pursuing your purpose, in chasing your dreams, and running your race. This type of preparation can be extremely difficult. A farmer must remove even good plants if he wants to dedicate the ground to coffee alone and there will be some good, or even great, things that have to be removed from your life if you want to make room to say yes to and pursue the best things.

I've had to do this a couple of times in my own life. Recently, I found myself in this position again. Throughout my career, I have always lived in this tension regarding my relationship with music. I love music. I love listening to it, I love creating it, I love leading worship, and even performing cover gigs. Songs have been known to make me cry because music seems to be my heart's primary language. Want me to remember something? Write a song about it. For a long time, one of my life's goals was to become a professional musician and I wanted it badly. I wanted to be on the big stage with the fog and the lights. I wanted to hear people cheering me on and singing my songs back to me. I wanted to tour the country on a smelly bus exploring new cities during the day and putting on great shows at night. This desire was so intense that I began to believe that any other path would mean that my life was nothing more than missed opportunities and unrealized potential. AKA, a complete and total failure.

I went all in. I started a band, wrote some songs, hit some open mic nights, and eventually booked a few gigs. Things were going really well when the first roadblock happened. Because of some relational drama and a couple of alcohol-charged arguments between two of my bandmates, the band broke up. I was a solo act again. Even still, I stayed the course. I stuck to my dream. I played solo gigs hoping to meet some other musicians with similar dreams to rebuild this thing and pursue that smelly tour bus. One night, I got what I thought was going to be my big break. A band that was recently signed to a major label was coming to town. They were touring in support of their debut album and needed an opening act. I got the call and jumped at the opportunity. In my mind, the story wrote itself. They would hear my music, we'd all become the best of friends, they'd invite me to open for them on the rest of the tour, my career would take off, and I would have my tour bus. That is not how the evening went. About

15 minutes before I was supposed to go on, my throat began to feel a little scratchy. By the time I took the stage, I was completely hoarse and could barely get the words out as I attempted to sing my songs. I fought my way through the 20-minute set while new waves of disappointment washed over me with every note I played. As I left the stage that night, three things happened. First, I felt my dreams being crushed once again. Second, my voice returned almost immediately. The third thing that happened was the headliners took the stage and put on an absolutely amazing show and no one in that room gave me another thought.

My relationship with music would continue in this way for years. I would get an opportunity that looked like it was going to be my big break only to have a door slammed in my face. Eventually, I came to terms with the realization that I wasn't created to be a professional musician. Even so, music remained a big part of my life for a long time. I got involved in the worship teams at my church and while I got a few opportunities to lead worship, I was most often playing guitar or drums. That finally changed at the church in which I currently serve. While it wasn't part of my job description, I was able to regularly lead worship on the weekends, in the youth ministry, and other events here and there. It honestly felt like a dream come true. To go from being rejected for years to finally feeling accepted and even sought after was, honestly, amazing.

Over the last few years, my role has shifted as I have grown. Growth always brings new responsibilities and increased demands on our time. As these shifts continued to happen in my career, I noticed that worship was beginning to become more of a distraction and a burden than a blessing. I still loved leading and playing music, but I couldn't help but think of all of the other places I should be or all of the other things that needed my attention. The things that were my responsibilities were regularly slipping through the cracks and I wasn't leading my team well. Finally, I received another promotion at my church and moved from overseeing our youth ministry team to overseeing both the youth and kids ministry teams. This has been such a blessing and I love what I get to do to impact the lives of the next generation. This change obviously came with new responsibilities and new opportunities. Translation: there was a larger demand for my time and it was becoming harder and harder to deliver my best.

I had to make a change. I tried backing down the number of weeks I was available to serve with the worship team. Eventually, I had stepped back to the point of being the "in case of emergencies" guy. Even then, it wasn't long before I knew I had to be done. I had to step away completely. In one of the hardest decisions I have ever made, I sold most of my guitars and music gear. Music would always be a part of my life, but "musician" would not.

Leading worship wasn't just a good thing that I did, it was a great thing that I loved. It got me excited, helped me experience God in major ways, and connected me with people as well. The decision to remove this part of my life wasn't one I took lightly. It was hard and it hurt a lot. But that decision has created so much more space for me to pursue the things that I have been uniquely created and purposed to do. I didn't realize it at first but playing music had become those weeds and rocks in the field of my life. God was trying to grow something new, but He couldn't until they were out of the way.

As I recall my own story, I think of a guy named Peter. Peter was a fisherman who had an encounter with Jesus that changed his life forever. In Luke chapter 5, Jesus is standing by a lake. A crowd of people is coming to hear him preach and they're pressing in on him. There are no microphones or stadium seats by this lake, so everyone is trying to get close enough to Jesus to hear what the teacher would say. That's when Jesus and Peter connect. Jesus asks Peter if He can use his boat as a temporary stage. Peter obliges and they push out into the lake a little to create a natural amphitheater. Jesus teaches the people from the boat and, when He finishes, tells Peter to "put out into deep water and let down the nets for a catch" (Lk. 5:4 NIV). Peter is tired and frustrated from a fruitless fishing expedition the previous night and doesn't seem interested. Besides, he's the expert here, maybe Jesus should stick to teaching. Peter says to Jesus, "Master, we've worked hard all night and haven't caught anything. But because you say so, I will let down the nets" (Lk. 5:5 NIV). Despite his exhaustion, he acquiesces to the request of Jesus and what happens next is truly amazing.

When they had done so, they caught such a large number of fish that their nets began to break. So they signaled their partners in the other boat to come and help them, and they came and filled both boats so full that they began to sink. When Simon Peter saw this, he fell at Jesus' knees and said, "Go away from me, Lord; I am a sinful man!" For he and all his companions were astonished at the catch of fish they had taken... (Lk. 5:6-10 NIV)

I wish I knew more about Peter's fishing career. I wish I knew if he was successful. Did people think of Peter as a great fisherman? Was business booming or was he struggling? I wish I knew if he felt like I did about music. Was fishing always his dream, or did he just inherit the family business? Was he constantly looking for his one big break? Did he have moments where it seemed like the business was going to take off, he was going to become a world-renowned fisherman, scale the business, (and the fish), and eventually franchise? I just don't know. But here's what I do know: the catch of fish they brought in that day was life-altering. Scholars have estimated this to be over 62,000 pounds of fish based on what is known about the style of the boats these fishermen used and their capacities. They go on to estimate the sale price of these fish to be between 700,000 and 1,000,000 denarii depending on the quality of the fish. For the four guys on the boats that day, the payout would have been between 12 and 36 years worth of their normal wages. If there was such a thing as a big break in the fishing business, this was it. But what happens next is truly remarkable. Scripture tells us that "Jesus said to Simon, 'Don't be afraid; from now on you will fish for people.' So they pulled their boats up on shore, left everything, and followed him" (Lk. 5:11 NIV).

I'm grateful that in my own life, my decision was made for me. My voice tanked and so did my opportunity to make it big. I can't help but wonder what would have happened if I had absolutely killed that night. What if all of my musical dreams were laid out right there in front of me and the headliners invited me to join them on tour? What if their label representative wanted to sign me on the spot? I know what would have happened: I would have jumped at the chance. I would have been on that bus faster than you can say "Grammy award winner Brandon Hair." Hey, it could happen. As I envision this, I also wonder what would have happened if, in that moment, Jesus approached me as I was about to get on that bus and said, "Come and follow me." That's the choice Peter faced. He wasn't at his lowest point feeling broken and hopeless. He was in a boat being crushed by the weight of his greatest success.

I can't say for sure what I would have done, one foot on that tour bus. But Peter chose Jesus. Peter would leave the fishing business that day and would go on to become Jesus' go-to guy, His right-hand man. Because Peter put down his nets, he got to experience closeness with Jesus, he got to witness miracles, he got to see lives change, and he got to be on the leading edge of this new movement that ushered in the redemption from sin, freedom from bondage, and peace with God. Because Peter gave up fishing for fish and went all in on fishing for people he got to step into his true purpose and become what Jesus described him as; "The rock on which [Jesus] will build [his] church" (Mt. 6:18 NIV). What a story, and what a life. Peter wasn't perfect. He made mistakes, he failed, he messed up, and he stumbled back into old patterns and old routines numerous times. But he never stopped pursuing Jesus and who Jesus called him to be. What crops have you planted in your life that are actually weeds, standing in the way of the true fruit you've been designed to produce? In addition to letting go of my music dreams, I had to make one other career-shifting decision: The day I knew my Starbucks career was over. I had stepped away from ministry to pursue that career and things were going really well. I loved Starbucks. I loved leading the team and I loved serving the customers that walked into my store. I was at the height of my career and I was making substantially more money than I had ever made before. Things were working and I had no plans to make a change. That's when I heard Jesus ask me to lay down my nets and follow him. It was difficult and painful. Leaving that store for the last time was honestly heartbreaking. It felt like I was walking away from an incredible story that I was co-writing with incredible people. But deep down, I knew it wasn't the story I was created to write.

I wish I could say that I went back to the church and "They all lived happily ever after," but to be completely honest, the next few years in ministry were some of the hardest years of my life. We'll get to that a little later in the book but suffice it to say, I was back in the correct genre, but still not writing the correct story. As difficult as that season was, it all led me to where I was designed to go. This was only possible because I was willing to walk away from something good knowing there was something great. I knew that my best 'yes' was still out there and I was committed to tracking it down.

Pursuing a life of purpose is a process. You won't wake up one day and discover that you've arrived. This process has many phases and many stops along the way. Don't get discouraged, don't get distracted, and lean into the process, knowing that if you don't give up, a delicious cup of coffee awaits. Also, purpose. The coffee is a metaphor.

So, whether you did or didn't buy a coffee farm, know there is so much to learn from the process. Accept that our stories, much like coffee's, are way better than we give them credit for. As you are by now well aware, this book isn't about coffee farming. It's about purpose, passion, Jesus, me, you, and how all of our stories tie together to make this beautiful picture we call humanity. This book is about the magic in the mug and how we can use that magic to help us discover the same magic within ourselves.

Let me ask again, what are you growing in your life that is in the way of what you could be cultivating? For me, it was music and coffee. For Peter, it was a fishing business. There are plenty of good things that can distract us if we're not careful. This sort of drift happens over time and often by accident. While it's not unheard of, we rarely drift into our purpose, usually, we drift away. Living our purpose takes intentionality. It takes planning and care. And it takes committing to be the person you were created to be. I am certain that if I stayed in the coffee business, I would have been successful by the world's standard. I am great at customer service, processes, and leading people. But God designed me for something different. So, like Peter, start this journey by clearing away the good; and maybe even the great, to pursue God's best for your life.

PLANTING, WHERE IT ALL BEGINS

"THE MAN WHO REMOVES A MOUNTAIN BEGINS BY CARRYING AWAY SMALL STONES."

—CHINESE PROVERB

No matter what you want your life to look like I'd be willing to bet it's not just going to happen to you. Your purpose or your dreams aren't going to just fall into your lap wrapped in a bow with a note that says, "You're welcome. And also, here's a puppy." The world just doesn't work that way and it probably won't on this side of eternity. The truth is all dreams have one thing in common: They take effort. They take dreamers who are willing to roll up their sleeves and get their hands dirty, who are actually willing to start. I don't know that this is contrary to popular opinion, but it is definitely contrary to popular preference. We see success stories plastered all over creation everyday of people who were nobody yesterday and a billionaire today. It's kind of nice to assume it just happened to them, because it means that maybe it might just happen to us. When success appears rapid it can seem like it came without a lot of hard work. But no matter how rapid their success may seem, these people accomplished their dreams by doing the same thing you and I must do. They took the first step. They acted and allowed their dream to move from a little cloud drawn above their heads into the real world, into something tangible. I don't know what your dream is, but I bet realizing it will require you to plant something. Whether it's an idea, a thought, a literal seed, or even a question. When you have a dream, step one is always to plant*.

Remember that coffee farm in Chapter 1? There's greatness buried beneath that surface, if only you can call it out. That trick, being able to see past what is to what can be is difficult for me. My wife, on the other hand, is very good at this. A few years ago, we were nearing the end of a lease agreement in the apartment we were living in, and we began to entertain the idea of buying a house. It was just outside of the market crash of 2008 and although house prices were starting to normalize, they were still fairly low and interest rates were pretty favorable. However, the area in which we were living and wanting to remain was still outside of our price range. It was going to be nearly impossible to find any house in that area, much less a house we loved.

Once we came to this realization our first instinct was to retreat and try to find another rental. But she didn't want to give up. She continued her search[+] and eventually found a townhouse on the market that was in foreclosure. She set up an appointment for us to see it and we went to take a look. When I walked through the door, I immediately thought I was being punk'd. The house smelled terrible as if decades of animal waste had gone unattended, the wood floors were in terrible condition, the countertops and cabinets were dirty and damaged, the layout wasn't anything like we wanted, and that was just my view from the front door. I was ready to leave before I had even made it through the foyer until my gaze made it to the back of the living room. I truly couldn't believe my eyes. Straight out of the back of the house was a view of the river across the marsh that could be enjoyed from the huge, screened porch that seemed to be inviting me to come and rest. All of a sudden, that dirty run-down house began to look ripe with potential. In an instant, I was able to see what my wife had seen all along. Because of that view I was finally able to hear my wife's ideas for turning this nightmare into our home. When that view was combined with her vision, I knew she was right; a little paint would brighten the place up, new countertops would make the kitchen warm and inviting, and new flooring would remove the lingering aroma left by years of neglect.

Over the course of a few months, we would paint, clean, scrub, demolish, refinish, build, and reshape this house into what it could be instead of accepting what it was. We bought it when it was a wreck because we were willing to put in the time and resources to bring out its potential. Today, it is a completely different house than the one we bought. I used to tell everyone we stole it because what it became was so much more than what I saw upon first view. I am so thankful that I allowed her to plant the vision of what this place could be in my heart and that together we worked to make that vision grow.

While this story sounds like an overwhelming success, it was one of the hardest things we have ever done. I told you the beginning and end of the story, but there was a lot in the middle. There were long days, late nights, disagreements, some of which turned into full blown fights, and even a moment where one of our children locked herself in her bedroom after spilling paint on the 2-day old carpet. We had to break into her room by picking the lock because she refused to face the music! Later that day, we took the lock off of the door completely.

FAILURE CAN BE THE MOST POWERFUL PART
OF SUCCESS IF WE ALLOW IT TO TEACH US,
DRIVE US, AND PUSH US TO BE BETTER.

Planting things is always difficult. There is an anxiety that comes with waiting. "What if it doesn't grow? What if I can't give it the attention it needs?" Just like the coffee farmer, there is a list of variables that we have to wrestle down if we're going to be successful planters. We must answer questions like "is it possible, does anyone care, are the conditions right, and am I willing to see it through?" Nothing made this truth clearer to me than trying to plant a vegetable garden while living in an apartment. This apartment had a small back porch and so I built a wooden planter box, filled it with dirt, and planted some seeds. My wife and I thought we could teach our daughter who was just under two years old at the time how to water the plants and let her learn some discipline and responsibility in the process. We planted quite a few things that were regular staples in our home like cucumber, bell pepper, and tomatoes. Then we prepared to never have to pay for vegetables again. Things went surprisingly well for a while. Before we knew it, we had sprouts! How exciting, we were gardeners. Nay, we were farmers! (You sang the song, didn't you?) We just knew that soon we would be providing vegetables to the whole community. Of course, soon we'd have to scale this thing and begin putting planter boxes in the woods behind the building. Who knows, from the humble beginnings of this one planter box we could be on the cusp of greatness.

Then we learned the next valuable lesson about gardening: Sprouts do not automatically become vegetables. Our plants started to grow but we had no actual idea what we were doing. The cucumber vines grew out of the box and across the yard threatening to engulf anything in their path. We tried to recover by putting a trellis in place, but it was too late. We never saw a cucumber. Not even one of the tiny ones that becomes a gherkin. The tomatoes ended much the same as we had nothing in place to support the growth of their vines. The peppers, which were planted in between the other two, never saw the light of day because apparently the proximity of one plant to its other plant friends really matters. This thing was a disaster. Needless to say, you won't be seeing any vegetables with my name on the label anytime soon.

Maybe not every idea is a great one that will turn into some legacy altering venture. But failure can be the most powerful part of success if we allow it to teach us, drive us, and push us to be better. My planting story wasn't a total loss. Through it I discovered that there are incredible farmers out there whose families I can support by buying their tomatoes at the grocery store and that there are plenty of fake plants out there that look real enough to make my office look lively. With these two truths in hand, it's easy to let the people with the real green thumbs do what they do best!

On the other hand, not every planting story withers. After remodeling the house, we truly felt like we had found a home. It was a place where we felt comfortable, safe, and connected as a family. We hosted friends for dinner, had life groups, birthday parties, play dates, and the list goes on. We made memories in that house, and they all stemmed from a vision that my wife and I planted together. Ultimately, we would sell that house and move out of state. That house very much helped to make our move possible. It all started by planting a seed of what could be.

On my visit to the coffee farm in Hawaii, I saw plants that were between 6 and 8 feet tall that were the result of years of care and attention. More than that, to me, they represented the realization of someone's dream. Someone was courageous enough to take the first step and buy some land. They prepared that land and planted a crop. They cared for it way better than I cared for my pathetic box garden. They had a big dream and went for it, not one time but over and over, consistently until that dream was a reality. We've all got big dreams. For some, it's to start a company. Others want to travel to faraway places. For others, it's to save the world by eliminating climate change or solving the global hunger crisis. We're all motivated by different things that make us want to succeed and all of our dreams are different. What they all have in common is that they stay dreams unless we move toward them. We have to take the first step.

The first step for a coffee farmer, looking at that prepared plot of land, is to plant the seed. Nothing happens unless he gets out in the field and does the hard work of tilling the land, planting, fertilizing those seeds, and helping them to grow. He has to commit to his craft and dedicate himself to seeing it through. This is especially true with a crop like coffee. Although most people think of coffee as a crop that grows on a bush, it actually grows on a tree. These trees can reach up to 100 feet tall and only produce fruit between the ages of 4 and 18 years of age. It makes the first step of planting much more difficult when you have a 4-year waiting period for return on investment. I've quite often wondered how one breaks into the coffee business. It seems like a huge up-front investment to have empty hands and pockets for the first four years.

While dreams can come upon us suddenly, we should avoid underestimating the time they take to prepare, to build, and to cultivate if we're going to bring them to fruition. We live in a culture where we expect a response to our emails within minutes, our pizza delivered in 30 minutes or less (preferably less) and our dreams to come true as soon as we wake up from the sleep which allowed us to have them in the first place. The upside of this culture is that information is literally at the ready for any skill we could ever hope to develop. We can watch a YouTube video and learn how to do anything short of open-heart surgery in minutes, we can watch college-level courses for free online, and we can be face to face with someone across the world instantly thanks to video calling and online meeting spaces. The world is literally at our fingertips 24/7 and all we really need to begin chasing our dreams is a willingness to be risky and take the first step.

The first step in any process usually contains equal parts of excitement and terror. We are excited about the potential that we see before us. Our imagination runs wild telling our hearts stories of our future success. We begin writing the story in our head as if it is already taking place and filling in the details of things like what our strategies and structure for weekly staff meetings will be even though we have no staff in place because we haven't actually done anything yet. We see pictures of ourselves making a difference, changing the world, and winning a Grammy. We start telling our family and friends about our dream, rarely stopping to think about how our plans might affect them and the stories they are writing. We often forget that maybe they have dreams that they are trying to make into a reality too. I know this isn't just me, right? Somewhere in all of this we hopefully come to grips with the fact that just talking about our dreams isn't going to get us anywhere; we actually have to do something. Right now, preferably. Suddenly, reality rudely comes upon us like a monsoon on our parade and reminds us of where we actually are: Nowhere. But, actually, we aren't nowhere. We are at the beginning. Every story ever written was an idea before there was ever a word on the page, and all of the stories we've told ourselves just haven't happened yet. We haven't gotten the job, or the girl, or the white picket fence, and certainly not the Grammy. What we've got is work to be done. We've got seeds to plant and growth to cultivate.

It's about this time, when we actually begin, that the fear sets in. The task at hand seems daunting. The thought that there could be months or years before we even see the seeds of our dreams begin to germinate and we know we're on the right track makes us second guess the whole thing. Will it be worth it? What if I put in these years of effort and end up with nothing to show for it? What if my fields stay barren and desolate? What if I end up destitute living in an alley with no friends and no way to check my Facebook feed? How am I supposed to know if people thought my cat video was funny? Then it happens, we find ourselves agreeing with the fear. We say, "You're right fear, it's not worth it. It's comfortable here. Big dreams are nice. Sure, there's potential, but it might never be anything more than that. There's nothing wrong with where I am. And who needs a Grammy anyway, it's just an award. If I stay where I am, at least I'll be safe." Nothing kills dreams faster than fear.

There's a story in the bible about a girl named Esther. She is a regular Jewish girl living under the rule of Xerxes. Xerxes is the powerful king of Persia who has a very beautiful wife, Queen Vashti. One night after the king and his friends have a little too much to drink, they begin to discuss Queen Vashti's beauty. In an effort to show how powerful he is, the king summons Vashti into the throne room and demands that she dance to entertain him and his company. Being a bit ahead of her time in the feminist movement she less than politely declines to acquiesce to his request. In order to save face Xerxes, "dismisses her from his presence." (Read: divorces her on the spot and banishes her from the kingdom.) Xerxes fairly quickly realizes he's not a huge fan of loneliness or public ridicule and decides to get himself a new wife. His advisors are sent out to find the most beautiful young women of the kingdom and bring them back to the palace for a beauty contest, winner gets to be queen. I imagine it to be sort of like The Bachelor without the... actually it was probably exactly like The Bachelor. Well, if the bachelor wasn't optional.

Esther is chosen as one of the contestants and reluctantly (read: she had no choice) goes to the palace to compete for the "love" of King Xerxes. Esther is found to be the most beautiful of the contestants and becomes Queen. She loves and serves her new husband and Xerxes grows to love and cherish Esther. Sometime later Esther is made aware by her uncle, Mordecai, of a plot by one of the King's advisors. This advisor, Haman, deceives the king into believing the Jewish people were plotting to rise against him. Haman convinces the King to decree that the Jewish people may be destroyed and that they are not allowed to defend themselves against this destruction[#].

Mordecai pleads with Esther to speak with the King on behalf of their people. There is a complication, though. In this culture the King's presence was an invitation only event. Not even the queen could go before the King unless she was summoned. Breaking this protocol typically had one of two outcomes; either your request was granted, or you were put to death. Esther is faced with a choice: she can stay safe in the care of the King, who likely doesn't know she Jewish, or she can take the first step and plant something great. Needless to say, Esther was afraid. She asked her people to pray and fast with her for several days. After that, she would approach the King.

For many of us our first steps toward greatness do not hold within them the balance between life and death, at least not in the physical sense. Knowing this, why do we allow ourselves to be paralyzed by fear? Maybe it's a fear of failure or a fear of rejection. For Esther it was a fear of death, both for her and the people she loved. Esther's choice to face her fear and approach the King was the right decision. She got her wish. She was able to save her people and Haman's true character was revealed. The King had him put to death for his dishonesty and Mordecai became his new official advisor. If Esther chose to play it safe an entire population of people could have been killed and God's story of redemption would have been forever altered. But here's the deeper thought. What if God was at work all along? What if God had a plan since before time began? The truth is that He was, and He did. God knew who Haman was long before anyone else did. He allowed Esther to rise to the position of Queen for such a time as this, this decision, and this moment. God started preparing her long before Queen Vashti refused to entertain the king and his friends, and when the time came, she was ready. She was ready to step into all God had for her. She was ready to take a risk and accomplish something amazing.

What if God is at work in your dreams, even though nothing has appeared above the soil yet? What if He has been preparing you for this moment all along? What if the experiences and situations you have been through were all in an effort to prepare you for one thing and now all you have to do is say yes? I believe that at some point all of us will face a decision that does hold within it the balance between life and death. It may be the decision you are facing right now. It may not involve a physical death of you or your loved ones, but maybe the death of your dreams and your greater story. The death of your part in God's redemptive story to the world. Your dreams matter. They are there for a reason. But whether they stay there or get released to make an impact is up to you. Releasing your dreams can be unnerving. It can be terrifying, but don't let it be paralyzing. Plant something great. Take the first step. If you don't, you're guaranteed to fail. But if you do, you get to anticipate the harvest. Greatness doesn't happen without that first step. Take it.

This is assuming you did the preparation. I suppose technically step 1 is preparation. But I can't go back and change that chapter now so let's assume you've done the research and are at the "this is what I am going to do" phase in our journey.

†It should be noted that my wife never stops scouring the internet for homes… like ever.

#If you are unfamiliar with the book of Esther, trust me when I tell you there's way more to this awesome story and you should definitely check it out.

CHAPTER THREE

HARVESTING, IT'S NOT JUST FOR ROBOTS ANYMORE

"THERE ARE TWO TYPES OF PEOPLE IN THE WORLD: PEOPLE WHO ADMIT HAVING SAID 'THERE ARE TWO TYPES OF PEOPLE IN THE WORLD' AND PEOPLE WHO ARE LYING ABOUT IT."

—ME

We've all attempted to categorize humanity by saying, "There are two types of people in the world...." If you haven't, then I am fairly sure you are lying. Does that offend you? Didn't you read the inspirational quote at the beginning of the chapter, where I said the same thing? Wait, are you... skipping the inspirational quotes? Quotes that I carefully selected (or just made up) for such a time as this? I... I think I'm offended. Definitely a lot to process. However, as I am a reasonably well-adjusted human adult who does not let every minor transgression devastate him, I shall forgive you. You're welcome. I know, I am so gracious. Let's start over.

When someone says, "There are two types of people in the world" they are usually trying to establish a dichotomy between two behaviors or points of view which can't possibly exist in one person. Usually, they themselves are firmly in one camp, regarding the other side with a hint of judgment. For example, "there are two types of people in the world: those who love babies and those who love axe murderers." Oh yea, I forgot to mention that often these quotes don't actually make any sense at all or even loosely relate to one another. Besides, there has to be some overlap in that one, right? I bet there are a bunch of people who love babies AND axe murderers. The point is, who doesn't love a good false dichotomy? Here's another one: "There are two types of people in the world: those who believe the end of the toilet paper should drape over the roll and psychopaths." Actually, that one is true.

Here's a dichotomy that isn't false at all. There are two types of coffee beans in the world: robusta and arabica. Robusta are the bottom shelf beans grown in less-than-ideal circumstances. These beans are cheap and easy. They're grown at lower elevations in flat fields that make harvesting easier and more convenient. The beans are slightly larger and boast more caffeine than their arabica counterparts. Their plants mature much faster and often produce more beans per plant than arabica trees. Robusta beans are also less susceptible to insects, pests, thieving birds, and adverse weather conditions. However, their overall quality is inferior to that of arabica beans. Because of this, they are popular in the cheaper grocery store and low-end coffee brands as well as many instant coffees and fast-food chains.

Arabica beans, on the other hand, are grown at high elevations. They require much more attention and care. These beans are far more susceptible to external conditions like bugs, pests, weather, and those evil birds*. Arabica beans are also much more difficult to harvest as they are grown in mountainous areas at elevations greater than 2,000 feet. Because of this, Arabica beans must be harvested by hand. Knowing all of that, it's easy to see why these beans carry a premium when it comes to price. Because of this premium price, they are typically reserved for premium coffees such as those found in higher end coffee shops, restaurants, and brands. The flavor housed within an arabica bean is much more complex and boasts a higher acidity level than robusta. All that to say, they're just better beans.

So, what can we learn from these beans? Lesson number one is if you're purely in it for the caffeine kick, save yourself some cash and start chugging that caffeine rich, flavor devoid, bottom shelf robusta. But, if flavor is what you seek, pony up for the rich, acidic, and complex magic of the good stuff!

More importantly, these two types of coffee teach us that we can have it easy, or we can do it right. Remember that house my wife and I decided to remodel? Well, we went all in. We bought the house, we made a plan, we hired a contractor, and we got to work. One of the projects we did was a major remodel of the master bathroom. Those home improvement shows would call it an 'en suite' because well, they fancy. Truthfully, I only added that fact because I want you to know that I too am fancy, but back to the topic at hand. We decided to completely gut this room. We removed the soaker tub and built a new all-tiled shower in its place. We installed a double vanity, moved the toilet to the opposite side of the room and we installed some built-in shelving in the corner where the toilet used to be. It was a major project. The last thing we did was take the old tile off of the floor and replace it with new, larger tile. Trust me, this was the right call. Removing old tile sounds fun at first. After all, there are sledgehammers involved! There is a sense of excitement and for a brief second you feel like Chip Gaines when he says with elation, "Demo Day!" Then, reality sets in and you realize that everything you Hulk-smashed to bits now has to be carried down multiple flights of stairs to the dumpster. As you are devising your plan for debris removal you learn that tile is heavy and makes even the sturdiest of trash bags rip open like a paper lunch sack after your juice box bursts inside. Even after all of this, you look at your ex-tiled floor to see there is still a long way to go. There are bits of tile and adhesive still attached to the floor which you have to scrape off piece by piece. And so, a cycle begins: Smash, scrape, stairs. Smash, scrape, stairs. Demo day may sound fun, but I assure you, it's not. Chip Gaines is a crazy person.

After several rounds of the "smash, scrape, stairs" process, our sub-floor still had some left-over bits of old tile, adhesive, and other debris that just weren't interested in being evicted. So, we came up with a plan. We decided to put plywood down to cover the old subfloor and then we laid the new tile on top of it. This is where things went a little sideways. See, we used 3/4' plywood that apparently had some kind of resin coating. This caused two extremely frustrating problems. First, it made the bathroom floor 3/4 of an inch higher than the bedroom floor, leaving an exposed plywood edge viewable from our bedroom, specifically in the line of sight from my side of the bed. This seems like a small issue, and it was, but it was a small issue like a paper cut is a small issue. It's tiny and not visible to most people, but to the person experiencing it, it is super annoying and way more painful than it should be. The second issue was that the tile didn't stick to the plywood as well as it should have. Because of this we had several tiles detach from the plywood. But hey, that was much easier than scraping that floor again or removing the old subfloor and replacing it! Eventually, this would result in more work but more on that later. For now, know that just like coffee beans, we can do things the easy way or the right way. Not both.[+]

When faced with a decision between the right way and the easy way I think back to the life of King David. At the time of this particular story, he would have been just David. At least, I think he would have been just David. It's hard to say, because he had been anointed to be the next king, but he still wasn't the actual king yet. A guy named Saul still had the job and while he had basically already been fired by God, he wasn't super willing to get off of the big chair and let his former servant sit in it. Maybe we can thank Saul for the existence of squatter's rights, but who knows. So, Saul does what any levelheaded, unemployed but won't leave the building, psychopathic, former but also current ruler would do: He gathers an army of 3,000 men and goes on a hunt for the guy who took his job. Never mind that he had been given that title directly from God Himself. You can't be replaced by a dead guy, was Saul's thinking.

In one such hunting trip, recounted in 1 Samuel 24, David manages to stay a few steps ahead of Saul and his army. Then, as Saul's army is beginning to close in, he suddenly decides - or maybe it was building up slowly since lunch, who can say - that he needs to relieve himself. So, he ducks into a cave to handle the business. It just so happens this is the very same cave in which David is hiding. Saul, being the master of situational awareness that he is, has no idea he is not alone and goes on handling the pressing matters of the moment. David's men whisper, "This is the day the Lord spoke of when he said to you, 'I will give your enemies into your hands for you to deal with as you wish'" (1 Sam. 24:4 NIV). Translation, "kill this dude so we can stop living in this cave that just became a bathroom."

After some thought, David decides to make his move. He sneaks up on Saul, gets right behind him, and cuts off his... robe. With his enemy in a completely vulnerable position, David literally cuts a fabric swatch.

Saul wraps things up and leaves the cave still having no idea that David (let alone all David's friends!) was even there. A few minutes later, David emerges from the cave with the swatch in hand and basically says, "get wrecked your majesty." That's it. Kind of anticlimactic if you ask me. This may give you cause to judge me, but I am a little impressed by David's level of pettiness here. Not exactly sure what that says about me as a person, but I am 100% "Team Swatch." Saul responds to David by basically saying, "Thanks for not killing me. In return, I won't kill you" And with that, Saul, and his army head for home.

Fast forward a couple chapters to 1 Samuel 26. Saul has apparently changed his mind regarding the whole "I won't kill you" situation and is closing in on David once again. They have found David's hiding spot and they are determined to end this. But, not before a good night's sleep. Saul and his army make camp and settle in for a few winks. Seeing this, David and one of his men sneak into the camp and make their way to the spot where Saul is sleeping. Saul's spear is in the ground right next to his head. One of David's soldiers, Abishai offers to "pin Saul to the ground." He knows David won't kill Saul and offers to carry that burden on David's behalf. (What a bro.) This sounds like a great deal if you're David. David, however, declines his thoughtful offer and then just kills Saul himself. Just kidding! He just takes Saul's spear and water jug. At this point, it becomes really easy to wonder if David actually wants to be king or if he just likes punking his former boss. David lets Saul live, and things play out pretty much the same as last time. Saul says "thanks" again and goes on his way. David has to know he'd be back.

Over and over again when David is presented with these opportunities, he opts not to take matters into his own hands. His logic is that it is God's job to sort things out. God anointed Saul and then anointed David. David understood that if he was to be king, it was up to God to make it happen. David had several opportunities to do things the easy way and help the process along. In fact, many saw these opportunities as God's way of making that happen. But David was convinced that the right way to become king of his people was to do so with clean hands. Eventually, David knew, God would deliver on this promise. And so, in 1 Samuel 31 Saul finds himself in a battle. He is surrounded and the enemy is closing in. Rather than get captured and subjected to whatever the Philistines would do to him, Saul falls on his own sword and takes his own life. When David hears of this, he actually mourns Saul's death. Shortly after this battle, David is finally named king of Israel.

THERE ARE NO SHORTCUTS ON THE ROAD TO MASTERY. EVENTUALLY, YOU ARE GOING TO HAVE TO DO THE HARD WORK.

When you are working toward your purpose and dreams, there will be days when you are tempted to phone it in, or to take the easy way out. In some of those situations your inner voice or the people around you may be shouting from the rooftops that this seemingly easy way is in fact God's provision. The question then becomes: Does this decision allow me to step into my calling the right way, with clean hands? Dreams and goals that are attained through shortcuts, underhanded tactics, or trickery are indeed often faster. They also tend to be empty and short-lived. Your calling deserves better than that. Your purpose is worth the hard work, effort, and the type of payoff that only comes through blood, sweat, and tears. The truth is there are no magic beans. (Except for coffee but we've already established that.) Want to lose weight? The answer is diet and exercise. Want to build a house? You're going to have to swing a hammer. Want to be an expert in your field? Experts say it takes about 10,000 hours of practice[#]. Want to write a book? You have to put your haunches in a chair and start putting pen to paper, or fingers to the keyboard.

While you may be able to fake it for a while, there are no shortcuts on the road to mastery. Eventually, you are going to have to do the hard work. The question is do you pay the price now or do you or wait until the easy way catches up to you? Eventually, we figured out a way to make the 3/4" plywood eyesore go away. I used a piece of wood trim to create a makeshift transition between the bathroom and the bedroom. It worked but it took a lot of frustration, a lot of complaining, and even a few stubbed toes to make it happen. Even though it would have required more "smash, scrape, stairs,", I can't help but think how much easier it would have been to do the floor properly from the start.

Don't get me wrong, the easy way may work for a while. I mean, the robusta bean farmers are selling their beans to someone. But you don't have robusta dreams, you have the good kind. You have arabica dreams. The kind that are cultivated high above the elevation of the average. You have talent, you have determination, and friend, you have what it takes. You have a story worth sharing and a gift worth giving. Great things are hard to accomplish. If they weren't, everyone would be doing great things and then they would be called average things. So, what's it going to be? Are you going to stick to the lowlands where mediocrity is abundant and easily accessible? Or will you do the hard work to climb high above the clouds and fight for the good stuff? Start climbing. I'll see you up there!

---

*I actually don't know if birds steal coffee beans, but I don't like or trust birds, they scare me. As such, I tend to believe at some level they are part of every problem coffee or otherwise.

†Unless it is. In which case, score! Check out the story of Naaman in 2 Kings 5. That guy got to take the easy way out in a big way!

#Random question, what exactly did those particular experts do for 10,000 hours to become experts in what it takes to become an expert?

CHAPTER FOUR

PROCESSING, WHAT TO DO WHEN THERE'S NOT A WRONG CHOICE

"NO ONE EVER MADE A DIFFERENCE BY BEING LIKE EVERYONE ELSE."

—BUCKMINSTER FULLER

For the coffee farmer, here's the situation: They planted their crop and have now harvested the coffee cherries. Still, they are actually quite a way from being ready for your morning pick me up. The next step in their journey is called processing. Processing is the means by which the green coffee "bean" is extracted from the "everything else" that makes up a coffee cherry. A coffee cherry is kind of like a peach in its structure. Unlike a peach where we eat everything and toss away the pit, in a coffee cherry, the pit is the prize. We toss away everything else in pursuit of that sweet, sweet treasure in the center.

There are three different ways coffee can be processed in order to remove the bean from the rest of the cherry. The first method is called 'Washed processing,' which uses a lot of water. First, the cherries are put in giant tanks called wet mills. Once there, the unripe cherries (aka the bad ones) float to the top and are separated from the ripened ones (aka the good stuff). Next the good cherries are depulped by giant machines that use friction to separate the bean from the outer parts of the cherry. Afterward the beans are put in fermentation tanks for 18-36 hours. This part of the process breaks down the mucilage (the remaining fleshy material from the outside parts of the cherry) from around the bean by using enzymes, a protein that speeds up chemical reactions. From there, the beans are laid out to dry for about 5 to 7 days. After they are dried the beans are rested while they continue to dry and develop flavors. This whole process can take up to two months! At this point, the rested beans are hulled, a process in which the parchment on the outside of the bean is removed. Finally, the beans are ready to be roasted.

This method usually produces more acidity than beans processed in other ways. Many Latin American countries use water processing and as such, the coffees of Latin American origin are typically noted for their higher acidity than Indonesian or African coffees.

"Semi-washed processing" is similar to washed processing with the exception of the fermentation process. Semi-washed coffees are de-pulped right after harvesting on the farm using small machines that are cranked by hand. Next, they are rinsed and shaken together to remove the mucilage, although some of the fruit stays behind contributing to the flavor of the final product. As the process continues, they are partially dried to reduce excess moisture. After all of this, the beans leave the farm and are transported to a milling station. The beans are then dried a little more, hulled, sent for final drying, sorted, and bagged for transport to a roasting facility. Coffees that are processed through this method typically have earthy or herbal flavors. Indonesian coffees typically go through this method of processing which is why they are the best*.

The final method is called "natural processing." It only has four steps making it the most resource efficient. In natural processing coffees are received at the processing location and laid out to dry on large drying racks. They are turned regularly over several days and become hard and withered like a raisin. Next, they are hulled through a process that removes the pulp, mucilage, and parchment in a single step. Finally, they are dried completely, bagged, and sorted for transport. These coffees get most of their flavor from the coffee cherry itself during the drying. Many African countries, Yemen, and Brazil are known to primarily use this method. While the flavors are a little less predictable because of their dependence on a high number of variables, these coffees typically have fruity flavor notes.

Ultimately, the processing method a farmer chooses isn't going to make or break their business. Similarly, most of the decisions we make aren't going to send us skyrocketing forward or crashing into a fiery blaze of destruction. As we pursue our dreams, plenty of decisions don't necessarily have a right or wrong answer. Instead, those decisions, like the different methods of processing coffee, influence where we are going to end up. The question is, "which of the likely outcomes gets me closer to where I want to go?"

As I learned more and more about the different processes on my own coffee journey, I started to wonder why certain regions chose one method over another. It didn't seem like there was a right or wrong way, just personal preference. The more I learned, the more I became convinced that each of these methods had great things about them as well as downsides. I learned, for example, that the availability of fresh water was often the primary driving factor in the decision of which method to use. This was especially true for countries like Ethiopia where clean water can be in short supply. These farmers and processing plants were opting to make the best use of the resources they had available. In essence the question as to which method to use boiled down to exercising the wisdom to use what they had.

Early in our relationship my wife and I had a minor conflict regarding a Christmas tree. The first thing you need to know is that we are "real tree people". I was recently offered a free fake pre-lit tree and I politely changed the subject so that this generous soul would not have to hear my rant on fake trees. But since I am sure you are dying to know my opinion, I grew up with real trees. I love the smell of them, I love the look of them, and I love the process of taking my family to pick out a real tree every year. Maybe your fake tree looks better than mine, but it also smells like a Wal-Mart stock room so there's that.

I will admit that real trees have some downsides: needles, sap, the possibility of catching fire and torching your home, and the potential for spiders. Fun fact, some Christmas trees have spider eggs in them that are supposed to hatch in the spring when it's warm. In related news, most homes feel a lot like spring to those dormant eggs. Good times. Even with all of these challenges, the biggest of these downsides has to be that you have to square the bottom of the tree to get it to stand up straight. Usually, you can get this done at the tree farm and it's fine but every now and then you get it in the stand and realize it's still leaning. As I am sure you have figured out, this happened to us one year. My wife and I went and picked out a tree from our local tree farm. They trimmed the bottom, and it looked pretty good. When we got it home, we realized that it was crooked. Not a little crooked but like really crooked. It leaned so hard that we were concerned it was going to fall over, break a few lights, catch fire, and burn our house to the ground. We had to fix it. That's when the real problem came. We realized that we didn't have the right tools for the job. I had a circular saw but what I really needed was a chainsaw or a reciprocating saw.

Obviously, the first step was to alert my wife to the situation and convince her to let me go buy a new saw. That wasn't going to fly as we were just starting out and the "new power tool" line in our budget was nonexistent. So, being the rugged and resourceful man that I am, I improvised. (Side note: never improvise when power saws are involved.) I used the circular saw and attempted to cut the bottom of the tree. Long story short: it did not work. The blade kept getting jammed as it wasn't a large enough blade to go all the way through the trunk of the tree. After a good half hour of fighting with it, all I had was a crooked tree with a random gash in the side. After some... intense fellowship I went into the garage and started digging through my tools. I found an old hand saw and started sawing away at the trunk. Here's what I learned: Douglas firs cut really easy. That hand saw went through that tree like a hot knife through butter. After what felt like hours of struggling with the circular saw, it literally took me seconds to level the bottom of the tree. After that, we got the tree secured and set up and I got a reciprocating saw for Christmas. Wins all around.

As I reflect back on that day, I realize that in the moment what I wanted was a new tool and to win an argument. While it was true that I did want to have the right tools for the job, the need for victory was the true driver. It turned out that I had what I needed all along. This reminds me of the story of Moses in the book of Exodus. Moses was a Hebrew boy who was born during a time of Egyptian rule and oppression. Through a series of God-ordained events Moses ends up being raised in the house of the Pharaoh as a member of the royal family. One day it all comes crashing down when Moses murders an Egyptian who is abusing a Hebrew slave. Moses is found out and has to run for his life. Suddenly this Hebrew boy who became royalty and was willing to fight for his people is on the run and hiding out raising sheep in the desert.

This could easily have been the end of Moses' story, but God intervened in a big way. One day as Moses was tending his flock, he saw a burning bush. What was strange about this bush was that while it was on fire, it was not being consumed. Naturally, Moses had to check it out. He approaches the bush and hears a voice coming from the on-fire bush that won't burn. Totally normal day. Turns out it is God who is speaking to Moses from the bush. He paints this picture of Moses' future. It is a future in which God will use Moses to lead His people out of captivity and into freedom in a land that they will finally be able to call home. This sounds amazing. I'd like to think if God told me I was going to do something great I'd respond positively and go after it with everything I have.

Moses doesn't do that. Instead, like me in my Christmas tree fiasco, Moses begins to tell God about all of the things he doesn't have. He starts with the heartbreaking question, "Who am I that I should go to Pharaoh and bring the children of Israel out of Egypt?" For someone who's familiar with the story, we read this and think, "What do you mean, 'Who am I?' You're Moses, man!" But Moses hasn't read this story yet. He has no idea what's going to happen next. When he looks at himself he doesn't yet see what we see. God responds with, "But I will be with you." Again, I'd like to think that'd be good enough for me. For Moses, it wasn't. He goes on to ask, "who should I say YOU are?" God then provides His resume, as if that was needed. Apparently "can appear incorporeally inside a burning bush that does not burn up" wasn't impressive enough for Moses. Moses again argues, "I'm not the guy, they won't believe me."

God then asks the question that we must all answer if we're to pursue our God-given purpose and dreams: "What is that in your hand?" This question must have been somewhat confusing to Moses because all he had in his hand was his shepherd's staff... a glorified stick. God tells Moses to throw it on the ground. Moses does and the staff turns into a living snake and back again. God then tells Moses to put his hand in his cloak. He does and when he pulls it out it is leprous. God tells him to do it again and this time Moses pulls his hand out completely healed. After all of this, Moses still gives yet another excuse. "God, I am not a good enough speaker. They won't listen to me." God says to him "I am the one who made man's mouth, I will speak through you. I will lead you." Desperate, Moses responds, "God, please send someone else." God makes what seems to be a compromise here and tells Moses that his brother Aaron will go along and be his mouthpiece to the people. Finally, Moses relents, goes home to his father-in-law, and tells him that he's going back to Egypt.

This story begins full of heartbreaking excuses and crippling doubt. Over and over Moses questions his value, his ability, and his calling. Again, I'd like to think that the burning bush would have been all the proof I needed. But Moses had excuses for literally everything God asked of him or called him toward. Haven't we all done this? God puts a big dream in our heart and gives us our own burning bush moment in which He seems to shout, "This is what I have for you!" It may even be crystal clear to everyone around us. Our friends, family, Facebook connections that we haven't spoken to in decades, and even some random strangers seem to confirm the dream and yet, we are still not quite sure. We fill our heads and our hearts with doubt. We let the voice of the enemy creep in, and he often begins this internal negative press conference with, "Yes, hello. Question for the dreamer: So, who exactly do you think you are? Like, what makes you think you're worthy of dreams like that?" This voice can be debilitating. Like Moses we say things like "my past is too broken, I don't have the skills, I don't have the experience, I don't have the influence, I don't have the credibility." And that infernal voice in our heads says

"AMEN! Louder for the brain cells in the back!" We let this voice grow louder and louder until it's the only voice we can hear. Meanwhile, the voice we should be listening to, the voice of the God who created us, who knows us, who loves us, and who put those dreams in our hearts for His glory and purpose, simply invites us to bring what we have and let Him use it for the benefit of His kingdom.

Friend, what is in your hand? If you will lay it at the feet of Jesus, He can use the ordinary things you bring to the table to point to His glory, to show His power, and to make His presence tangible in the lives of those around you. If you will give Him your hands, He can use them to serve His kingdom, to bring healing into the lives of the hurting and the broken, and to be a physical representation of the love our Father has for His children. What our friends in the coffee business have figured out is that it is not about the things we don't have. It is about using the gifts we've been given in service to our purpose. The natural processors don't get discouraged by the lack of water around them. Instead, they lean into the resources that are available and celebrate the unique flavors that come from their surroundings. What we have in our hands? Questionable. What we have in God's hands? More than enough.

> SOMETIMES ALL WE NEED IS WHAT WE ALREADY HAVE.

When now-obedient Moses arrived back in Egypt, Pharaoh immediately let the people go. Just kidding. That's actually the point when things got really hard for Moses and the children of Israel. Pharaoh was less than willing to let the people go. Moses was asking Pharaoh to release his entire workforce. A workforce that cost him zero dollars in salaries or benefits because they were all slaves. Pharaoh actually increased their workload and made conditions even worse in response to Moses' request, so much so that the people he was there to free asked him to leave. It took God bringing ten plagues upon Egypt for Pharaoh to relent and let the people go. Finally, Moses was able to lead the people out of Egypt and begin their journey to freedom.

When I finally searched through my garage for a better way to level that tree, I realized I had a tool that could do the job. It was there all along, but I was so caught up in what I didn't have, that it blinded me to what I had the whole time. Admittedly, cutting the bottom off of a Christmas tree is not quite as difficult as leading a few hundred thousand of your closest friends on a decades-long journey through a desert. But what we can learn from both situations and our friends who process coffee is this: sometimes all we need is what we already have. God is intentional, thoughtful, and efficient. He is not wasteful, and He is not random. He has given you gifts, talents, relationships, experiences, and dreams that all point you toward your purpose. Moses had riches and royal authority, but all he really needed was the stick in his hand to pursue what God called him to do. Thousands of years later, Moses is still recognized as one of the greatest leaders to have ever walked the earth. Throughout the rest of scripture, he is mentioned again and again as one of the fathers of the nation of Israel and a hero of the faith. All because he used what he had, a stick and a story, and allowed God to take it from there.

Let me ask you again, what do you have in your hand? Are you willing to give it to God and let Him change it, shape it, and send it? If so, you're well on your way to a life that is full of purpose and passion. Don't let what you don't have dictate who you are and what you are capable of. Let God multiply your gifts and use them to bring light to your world.

This is my own personal opinion. Feel free to disagree. It's ok for you to be wrong.

CHAPTER FIVE

BOOM, ROASTED

"WHAT MATTERS MOST IS HOW WELL YOU WALK THROUGH FIRE."

—CHARLES BUKOWSKI

After planting, harvesting, and processing we finally come to the part where coffee achieves the form we know and love. Until this point, it has been something that most people would not recognize. From a seedling to a tree to what looks like a cherry, the coffee is finally processed into something that looks like a peanut. Coffee is kind of like an unconfident teenager that keeps reinventing himself in hopes of finding his identity in the right social group. Thankfully, coffee avoids the Axe body spray phase, or the "sit moodily with a guitar in the corner at parties" phase. Now, it's reached the point where it transforms into the dark aromatic bean we look forward to seeing every day. It's finally going to find its true self. Probably on a backpacking trip in Europe during a gap year. Just kidding. It's much simpler than that. All our coffee has to do to become this beautiful, flavorful, dare I say magical bean, is hang out in a 400-degree furnace for a couple of minutes. It's time for our coffee to get roasted.

Roasting coffee is an art form. If you roast it too little, it won't have much flavor at all and in fact, it may not even grind properly because there is too much moisture within the bean. Roast it for too long and... well, let's talk about how lovely the aroma of burnt popcorn is*.

On my trip to Hawaii, I had an up-close opportunity to learn about roasting coffee. As I toured the coffee farm, I actually got to roast some of my own coffee beans. The roaster who showed me how the process worked was also preparing to defend her title as the top roaster on the island that coming weekend in some sort of coffee Olympics. What I'm saying is she was kind of a big deal. The more I learned about the roasting process, the more I thought, "Wow, that sounds really painful and extremely unpleasant."

Here's how it works: First, the roaster is heated to about 385 degrees. Then the green coffee beans are put inside the massive oven for their short tanning session. As the roasting begins, moisture is forced out of the beans, and they begin to dry out and expand in size. Some of the sugars inside the beans are forced out and converted into gas. While most of the sugars are forced out, some remain in the bean and are caramelized. The caramelization of these sugars is what gives the roasted beans their flavor profiles. The more these sugars caramelize the more intense or dark the flavor becomes. As the roasting process continues, the beans turn from green to yellow and eventually begin steaming as they release more and more moisture. As the extreme heat continues to do its work the beans crack resulting in a loud popping sound. At this point the beans are somewhat palatable and useful for drinking but, if the process ended here, the flavor would be pretty weak.

The roasting continues and the sugars continue caramelizing as the beans themselves get more and more airy and lightweight, while at the same time growing larger. After a bit more roasting, the beans approach a second crack and a louder and more violent popping sound occurs. They continue to develop darker, richer flavors as the sugars that remain continue to caramelize and sink deep into the bean. Here, the skilled roaster removes the beans and moves on to the next step. But for the novice, the potential is there to over roast their once beautiful beans, scorching them and turning the pleasing and vibrant aroma to something burnt and offensive.

Even though the beans are roasted, they're not quite done. During the roasting process, the beans shed their exterior shell leaving behind chaff. This chaff must be removed from the beans so that it doesn't become part of your next cup of Joe. The process of chaff removal is simple. The beans are shaken back and forth between strainers and the chaff is sifted out. Once the roasting and chaff removal is done, the beans are rested and cooled until they are ready to be packaged or stored for use.

This sounds intense but the roasting is where much of the flavor of our coffee comes from. And at the end of the day isn't the flavor what it's all about? I mean sure, most coffee drinkers are probably already addicted and if delicious full-flavored coffee weren't available, they'd opt for the closest caffeinated beverage in order to avoid being reduced to a decaffeinated zombie-like shell. For the rest of us, flavor is a big deal and for coffee, the depth of the flavor is directly correlated to how much time it has spent in the fire.

I think you see where I'm going with this. If you look at history, people who do great things first experience trials and difficult situations firsthand. When I think about hard times, I quickly think about someone like Bethany Hamilton. She was a Hawaii native who grew up on a surfboard. She was a surf prodigy and was gaining recognition in the sport by the time she was thirteen. Things were falling into place for her until one day out on the ocean she was attacked by a shark, severing one of her arms at the shoulder. Bethany's friends were able to help her get to the shore but by the time she got into the ambulance she had lost nearly sixty percent of her body's blood. Through God's grace and some great medical care Bethany would survive.

If I were Bethany, I doubt I'd ever even walk through a puddle again, much less get back in the ocean. When I was about 10, I was stung by a jellyfish and it took a lot of convincing for me to even go back to the beach, much less get in the water. But just twenty-six days after the attack, Bethany was not just back in the water but back on the board. She refused to live her life in fear or let this tragedy define her. Her determination paid off. Just two years after the attack that took her arm, Bethany won first place in the NSAA World Championships. In 2017, Bethany was inducted into the Surfers Hall of Fame. Now, a mother of three boys, Bethany continues to surf and to compete and she uses her platform to share the love of Jesus with those around her.

There are countless stories of people who find greatness and purpose on the other side of pain. Stories of people who have weathered the storms of life, who have spent time in the furnace and come out on the other side. Many have been through trials so difficult that they thought they were going to break. They heard and felt that violent cracking and thought they were going to be ripped apart. Instead, they came out a little lighter, a little larger, and with a flavor of their own that they could offer to the world around them.

For some, they made it beyond this moment only to find themselves in a new fire. Still under pressure and approaching a louder and more violent breaking point, survival seems unlikely. The fire is too hot, the situation is too hard, they can't possibly make it to the other side. Then, something happens. That loud cracking and popping happens and yet, they find themselves still standing. This time, that unique flavor that was, at one point, barely developed is now fully formed. They have learned who they are and what they were put on this earth to do.

Sometimes we get to the end of our rope and we find ourselves in a season that we know we can't survive. But then something happens. We get pushed beyond the breaking point and find out that on the other side, we're still here. We're still alive. We're going to make it. Those seasons are hard. They hurt. They make us bleed. They make us feel bruised, broken, and defeated. But they also pull things out of us that we didn't know were in there. Just as the coffee bean expels gas and unnecessary sugars as its flavors are refined and developed, we are refined in the fires of life. We are made better, more complete. We've lost the useless chaff and are more capable than we were before.

About three years ago, I got really into running. I wish I could say I was still killing that game and racking up those miles, but alas. I got out of the habit, then out of shape, and now I am at the phase where the main running I do is with my mouth as I continue to make up new excuses. But back to when I was in my "prime." After doing some 5ks and a few 10ks, I decided to train for a half marathon. Running a 5k isn't too bad; if

I really wanted to, I could probably do one right now. I wouldn't be fast, I wouldn't enjoy any part of it, and I would be in a decent amount of pain after it was over, but I could pull it off. A 10k on the other hand, that would take some work. Now, double that and we're at a half marathon and there is no way I would even think of doing that without training for quite some time.

But back then I was training regularly and working toward that goal. What I learned is that there are several barriers that you have to clear to run a half marathon. For me, jumping from a 5k to a 10k wasn't too bad but getting past the 10k was extremely difficult. Breaking that six-mile barrier took a lot of work. I still remember the first time that I ran seven miles. It was a huge milestone. I think I cried but not from the pain. After that, came the ten-mile barrier. For weeks I was maxing out at eight and a half, nine, nine and a quarter, eight again, nine again, a week or two of three to four mile runs that were incredibly frustrating, and finally, ten point one. Like that six-mile wall, I thought it was impossible. There were days I could feel my body giving up. I just knew I would never get past ten miles and if I couldn't do that, the thirteen point one mile half marathon would never happen. After I finally broke that ten-mile barrier, the remaining three miles were nothing. I crushed them. There will be times when you think you have nothing left, that the pain is too great, and the tank is empty. When you find yourself in these seasons, just don't quit. Stick to the game plan, keep working, keep going, maybe take a break and then come back to it. Just maybe don't take a three-year break. It doesn't usually work like that. What I am saying is, don't give up when things get hard, there is more in you than you think.

In Daniel chapter 3 we find the story of Shadrach, Meshach, and Abednego. They have been taken captive by the Babylonian King, Nebuchadnezzar (I refuse to keep typing that whole thing. Let's call him Chad) and conscripted into royal service. At first, it seems like it could be a pretty sweet deal, well, minus the whole captivity part. A little later, we learn that Chad has a bit of a God complex, so he constructs a golden idol and says that at the sound of the instruments, everyone is to bow down to this idol in worship. The decree also states that anyone who refuses to bow down will immediately be thrown into a blazing furnace. No take backs, no re-dos, do not pass go, do not collect $200. This was a bit of a problem for our captive friends because they were Israelites who served the Lord. And right at the top of God's top ten, "Thou shall have no other gods before me."

Translation: people of God, don't bow down to that gold thing. It's not a real god. So, Rach, Shach, and Ab (as their friends probably called them) decided to stick to the plan of the true God and not bow to the gold statue. The day goes on, they have their plan, and then... it's time to face the music. Literal music. Loud music plays throughout the land indicating that the time has come to bow down to this fake god. Well, our friends stick to the plan. Not Chad's plan, their plan, the "how 'bout we just don't" plan. They do not bow. This act does not go unnoticed. Someone sees them and decides to try and gain some favor from King Chad by selling out Rach, Shach, and Ab. I guess they didn't know that snitches get stitches in the real world!

Well, King Chad is obviously furious and in true "crazed dictator with a god complex" fashion, demands our friends appear before him forthwith. Enraged, Chad asks, "are you guys for real right now? Don't you know what I'm going to do to you?" He restates his entire diabolical plan about the furnace and the burning, as any villain would, and finishes it with, "What god will be able to rescue you from my hand?" Spoiler alert, there is one God capable of such a feat. Let's keep going shall we.

Shadrach, Meshach, and Abednego answer King Chad. They say something to the effect of, "Yeah, we're for real. We know about the plan, the furnace, the burning; we're aware of all of that. The thing is, we're not really that scared of you. See, we serve this god, well he's actually The God. The one who created all of this, and you as a matter of fact. We serve that God, so we are going to go ahead and opt out of the 'bowing down to the false one's' plan that you seem to be peddling. We know that the God we serve is going to rescue us from your hand and use our story for His glory. So, where's this furnace? Oh, and by the way, even if God doesn't rescue us, we will never bow down to you or your false Gods." (Mic drop).

Chad is not impressed. He resolves to make an example of these three young men and orders Shadrach, Meshach, and Abednego to be restrained. Next, he orders the furnace to be heated to seven times its normal temperature. And so, it goes. As the guards approach the furnace and throw our hero's in, the flames are so hot, that the guards drop dead as Shadrach, Meshach, and Abednego fall in. A few minutes go by, and King Chad goes to check on the progress of this roasting. To his amazement he sees four men walking around in the fire. King Chad is obviously confused. He asks, "Didn't we throw three men in the fire? What's up with the extra dude wandering around in there? Follow up question, how are they walking around in there instead of being, you know, DEAD?"

The answer was simple really. Shadrach, Meshach, and Abednego were right. The God they served was capable of rescuing them. And He did. Incredibly though, God didn't delegate this rescue to an angel, or use His cosmic powers from afar; He stepped down out of heaven to walk through the flames with them. Scripture tells us that when Shadrach, Meshach, and Abednego came out of the furnace, they were so not burnt that the smell of the flames wasn't even on their clothes. Here's what I know about fire. If someone starts a campfire within 63 miles of me, I will smell like smoke for a month and a half. These guys literally walked through the flames and didn't even smell!

I'd be willing to bet that for Shadrach, Meshach, and Abednego, the metaphorical roasting process didn't actually take place in the furnace. I'd bet for them the true pressure test was found in the moments leading up to the furnace. First, the decree was issued from Nebuchadnezzar that when the band plays the people bow. That brought with it a little heat and a little pressure. They had to decide right then what they were going to do when the situation arose. They decided they would not bow. Maybe some of their other friends thought they were crazy. Maybe some of the Babylonians threatened to alert the authorities. But until the music played, the harm was still theoretical.

Then the day comes. The music plays. It's time to bow down. The heat and the pressure increase. Will they break? They have to evaluate the cost. Will standing for the God they serve be worth it? It's in these moments that the things that aren't important to us are stripped away. Just like gasses and sugars are expelled from the coffee bean, the insignificant stuff fades away and we're left with only the most important pieces. There are violent threats and deadly consequences but they remain standing and we hear that first "crack." They come out on the other side of this first test stronger and with greater resolve.

Then, they're summoned before the King. Suddenly the pressure and the (now literal) heat are turned up as Shadrach, Meshach, and Abednego have another choice to make. Do they fold or do they double down, stick to their convictions, and end up ashes? Surprisingly, they are presented with a way out. The King basically says, "Hey guys, the rule says when the beat drops so do you. If you can agree to do that from now on, I'll let this one slide." Is this their chance to escape? They have to make another decision. Take the deal, step out of the pressure, and get out of this thing alive or trust God in an impossible situation. The outrage, the threats, and the reality of their situation has become louder and more violent. The question had to come to mind, is God going to deliver us? They didn't have Paul's writing to tell them that, "to live is Christ, to die is gain," or a Philippians 4:13 bumper sticker to convince them they would be fine. All they had was a conviction that their God was THE God and serving Him was all that mattered. They decided to trust God and – CRACK – they found their flavor. They survived the second threat, went confidently into the fire, spent some time in the physical presence of the Lord in and came out on the other side.

The closest I've ever come to being set on fire is the time that I actually set myself on fire. Thankfully it was one of those flash situations because I had a very small amount of gasoline on my bare foot and the gas burned off long before I actually felt the heat. But I was 9 years old, unsupervised, and dude, I just set myself on fire. A close second is the time I had shingles. Shingles is a remnant of the chickenpox virus that lies dormant in your body just waiting to pounce. It attacks the nervous system and, in my experience, feels like a combination of a really bad sunburn and a tiny hurricane living in my lower back. While antiviral meds, creams, and lotions can help a little, ultimately the virus has to "run its course." Throughout the experience, there were many sleepless nights, uncomfortable days, and what felt like spontaneous lighting strikes happening inside of my body. Needless to say, the experience was not my favorite.

I remember asking a lot of "why" questions during this time, but mostly, why is shingles a thing? I am confident that a science-based answer exists, but I don't care about that answer. The answer I want is basically "Why are there bad things?" Why did these men have to face a crazed dictator and a fiery furnace? Why did Bethany Hamilton get attacked by a shark? Why do I have to deal with shingles? But what if instead of asking why suffering happens, we asked, "What can I do with this suffering?" or, "What can I learn from my time in the fire?"

Friend, at some point we'll all spend time in the fire. The question is, do we trust God to walk through it with us? Do we know that the Lord is good and capable and willing to deliver us from it? And do we trust Him enough to say that even if He doesn't, we still refuse to bow to the things of this world or give up in the face of difficulties? There will always be an easy way out, a King Chad who dangles success or power in order to get us to compromise our convictions. There will always be that compromise that allows us to sacrifice our values on the altar of comfort. Shadrach, Meshach, and Abednego could have simply bowed. They could have denied their defiance or even played dumb to the King. He offered them these outs. They could have taken any of these easy exits instead of stepping into the fire and seeing what God could do with their lives. But they did not bow, and that decision changed everything.

YOUR CHARACTER WILL REMAIN LONG AFTER
ANY PLATFORM YOU REACH FADES AWAY.

King Chad, amazed, approached the furnace (probably with extreme caution as not to meet the same untimely fate as his henchmen) and called out to Shadrach, Meshach, and Abednego saying, "servants of the Most High God, come out! Come Here!" After standing by in astonishment for a minute or two, Chad says this in Daniel 3:28-30:

> *"Praise be to the God of Shadrach, Meshach, and Abednego, who has sent his angel and rescued his servants! They trusted in him and defied the king's command and were willing to give up their lives rather than serve or worship any god except their own God. Therefore, I decree that the people of any nation or language who say anything against the God of Shadrach, Meshach and Abednego be cut into pieces and their houses be turned into piles of rubble, for no other god can save in this way." Then the king promoted Shadrach, Meshach, and Abednego in the province of Babylon.*

Shadrach, Meshach, and Abednego stuck to their convictions and as a result the kingdom of God was advanced and Shadrach, Meshach, and

Abednego were promoted to a position of high authority and honor. I'm not promising that what happened to them is what will happen every time. Unfortunately, sometimes you end up getting burned. Those times are painful and leave scars. Shadrach, Meshach, and Abednego were willing to suffer if that was God's will. To them, the outcome wasn't nearly as important as their character and their ability to shine a light for the Lord. Friend, let me encourage you that your character will remain long after any platform you reach fades away. Are you willing to walk through the fires the world demands you walk through, are you prepared to refuse to sacrifice your character and calling on the altar of comfort? If so, you might just develop that perfect flavor to share with the world and shine a little more light into the darkness.

If you like the smell of burnt popcorn, you are a monster.

CHAPTER SIX

PACKAGING, THE HOLE IN YOUR COFFEE BAG

"WHO AM I IF I DON'T HAVE WHAT IT TAKES?
NO CRACKS, NO BREAKS."

—LUISA (ENCANTO)

At this point in the process the coffee finally looks like those beautiful, delicious, life-giving beans we all know and love. It's been planted, harvested, processed, and roasted. Now, there are barrels and barrels of those sweet, sweet beans, ripe with potential. So, where do we go from here? Easy. They get bagged up and shipped out to stores, coffee shops, and restaurants. While this sounds easy enough, there is a pretty significant problem standing in the way: Gas, and a lot of it.

Over the next several weeks, those beans will release large amounts of carbon dioxide. If they are placed in a sealed bag the gas causes pressure to build. If this pressure is not released within a few days the bag will burst, and that would be sad. All that unrealized potential. There is good news: the gas is a temporary problem. Over the course of about a week, all of the built-up carbon dioxide is released, and the aforementioned beans no longer present a danger to themselves or others.

It would seem that the simple solution here is to let them rest in an open-air sort of situation for a week or so while they work out their internal issues. However, as we mentioned earlier, coffee is a beautifully complex creation and, in keeping true to itself, there can be no simple solutions when faced with logistical complications. The problem is that if the beans are simply left to sit out in the open they will go stale and your delicious cup of Joe will quickly become more of a "thanks, but no."

In the past, this problem significantly limited the coffee industry by making it nearly impossible to ship fresh coffee over great distances. While some solutions were attempted along the way, none allowed the gasses to escape the bag while also protecting the beans from oxidation and thus preventing them from going stale.

Thankfully, in 1960, an Italian packaging company called Goglio created a solution that would change the industry and make those coffee of the month clubs possible. They created a one-way degassing valve that would allow carbon dioxide to exit the bag while preventing outside air and contaminants from entering and causing staleness. Suddenly, a whole new world of possibilities opened up. Thanks to this simple valve, every coffee producer could finally ship their prized beans over massive distances all while ensuring freshness for the consumer. Wins all around! Now, coffee that was produced in Seattle could be shipped to the Carolinas or even worldwide. Farms in remote areas could now enter into the global roasting game and sell their coffee direct to consumers. While this certainly benefited the big bean guys, smaller coffee companies were now able to distribute their products farther and wider despite their lack of multiple roasteries, large warehouses, national distributors, and large farms. This small innovation made an incredible impact on the industry and allowed consumers to experience flavors and products that would have previously been limited to locals and tourists. The principle was simple: find a way to release the pressure, block out the contaminants, and keep what matters in the bag. That small principle may be worth the price of admission, or the price of this book, or both if such a situation happens to exist. But what does all of this gas talk have to do with achieving my dreams and living my purpose?

At some point in your life, there has been a situation, a circumstance, a comment, an assessment, or even a tweet about you that wasn't exactly helpful. In the moment maybe it doesn't seem like a big deal so, you bury it. You hide it deep down inside and think, "that'll be safe in there." Maybe you're right. But over time, those comments, situations, and circumstances begin to pile up. As they pile up, you begin to feel this overwhelming pressure to prove them wrong, rise above, or outperform the expectations of the peanut gallery. Eventually, the pressure builds up and reaches a point where it threatens to wreck us. You, like those freshly roasted coffee beans, need to find a way to de-gas, to process the pressure, release it, and move forward. If we don't, we're headed for an explosion.

How we handle pressure will be a major determining factor in our ability to pursue our dreams and purpose. I don't often make guarantees but here is one that you can take to the bank: if you're doing anything worthwhile, you will experience pressure. I recently saw the movie Encanto and immediately identified with Luisa. If you haven't seen this movie or don't remember who Luisa is, she's the strong one. She wasn't nervous. Additionally, she's as tough as the crust of the earth is. She was gifted with super strength, and she would use that super strength to help people in the town solve their strength related problems. She was constantly being called upon to rescue large animals from precarious situations, remove obstacles such as boulders from roadways, and even relocate entire structures from one spot to another. Luisa never failed. She was perfect in her ability to perform these tasks, but this perfection led her to experience overwhelming pressure. And so one day, when her gift started to disappear, the pressure to perform forced her to question her identity and value.

I identified with this pressure on such a deep level that even hearing her song on the soundtrack would often make my eyes sweat. At the time, this soundtrack was 100% of my daughter's preferred playlist so I only had to hear it every morning before going to work. The pressure to perform and to be perfect was so heavy that I physically felt like I was carrying a large boulder everywhere I went. To make matters worse, I didn't feel like there was anyone in my life who would understand and walk with me through that pressure. I, like Luisa, suffered in silence under the crushing weight of that very real but also imaginary boulder. It would take me months to unpack why I was experiencing this pressure. Unlike Louisa, the pressure that I was facing was completely self-inflicted and self-perpetuating. There was no one in my life that expected me to be perfect or to live up to these unrealistic ideals except for me and my internal voice. That internal voice guy is a real jerk sometimes. Like those early coffee bags, the pressure was coming from within and I did not have a healthy way to release it.

Pressure is nothing new and is not unique to me. Throughout scripture, history, and our own experiences, pressure tends to find a place in the center of our stories on a regular basis. The truth is that pressure will be a regular occurrence for as long as we live on this side of heaven. Pressure isn't really the problem, though; it's how we deal with the pressure – or refuse to deal with it – that determines where we go when it shows up. When I think of pressure, I often think of Daniel. Daniel was one of those Israelites who was taken into Babylonian captivity during the reign of King Nebuchadnezzar. This is the same Nebuchadnezzar we discussed in chapter five. The first thing the Babylonians sought to do with these newly arrived captives was assimilate the best and brightest of Israel into the Babylonian culture. They would basically wine and dine these kids and make them think that the Babylonian way of life was better than the old way. The goal was to completely erase the culture of the occupied nation as if they never existed. With the captive's culture extinct, it became way less likely that they would unify and rise up against their captors. In a move toward this cultural extinction, Daniel, whose name meant, "God is my judge," had his name changed to Belteshazzar which translated means, "Bel will protect." This Bel was a pagan god of the Babylonians. The intent was to disconnect Daniel's identity from the one true God and link it to this pagan god instead. The Babylonians goal of indoctrination was often quite successful until the day God got involved.

After the name change, next on the assimilation list was food and drink. Daniel and the other captives were given a daily portion of food from the king's own table, a reminder that they were favored captives who might yet find a special place in Babylon. Offering captives this privileged place in their new society was an effective way of encouraging them to abandon their old culture. The problem with this food was that most of it would have been considered ceremonially unclean to any Israelites. Just like their new names, these foods were chosen with the deliberate purpose of erasing the Israelite culture. Partaking was not presented as optional and thus Daniel faced extreme pressure to conform and to become like the Babylonians. However, "Daniel resolved that he would not defile himself with the king's food" (Dan. 1:8 NIV). Daniel approached those in power and asked for permission to stick to his traditional diet. With much reservation, his captor (who would be on the hook if Daniel and his friends became malnourished) agreed to experiment. Eventually, the Israelites are found to be healthier than those who ate from the King's table. Additionally, when they were presented to the King to be examined, they were found to have more wisdom and understanding than all of the captives who had eaten from the King's table. Because of this, Daniel gained some favor with the king and others in authority. But not everyone was happy with Daniel's success.

One night, our good friend King Nebuchadnezzar had a disturbing dream. Full of fear and anxiety, the king demanded that his wise men tell him the meaning of the dream. However, in order to make sure his wise men really knew what they were talking about, and not just telling him what he wanted, he demanded they tell him the content of the dream and its meaning. In essence the king wanted someone to read his mind, interpret the dream, and make it all better. Of course, his magicians told him that this was impossible. They argued that no man would be able to guess the contents of the king's dream. Instead of listening to reason, Nebuchadnezzar doubled down and condemns all of his wise men and magicians to death, including Daniel and his friends. As a result of this decree, Daniel and his friends were casually invited by Arioch, the captain of the guard, to head off to the gallows. Daniel calmly asked Arioch why he was receiving such an invitation and Arioch explained the whole situation. Daniel then asked Arioch to give him some time and promised that after such time, Daniel would do everything the king was asking. Arioch presented this idea to the king and while Nebuchadnezzar believed Daniel was merely stalling, the king reluctantly agreed to give him some time. With a few days to figure it all out, Daniel and his friends immediately went to God in prayer seeking wisdom, discernment, and rescue.

As God does, He shows up on behalf of His people. God reveals the dream to Daniel and gives him a full understanding of its meaning. Daniel approaches the king and tells him that his magicians are right, no man can reveal his dream. However, Daniel says that while no man is capable of such a feat, there is a God who can and has revealed that dream. Daniel then shares the dream in extremely accurate detail, along with its meaning. The king is astonished. He immediately promotes Daniel to a high-ranking position and declares the God of Daniel to be the one true God. While the dream and what it means is an awesome prophecy and a really cool moment in scripture, that's not the point here. Go read it sometime. For us, we're talking about standing up to and dealing with pressure.

NEVER LET THE PRESSURE OF CULTURE
CHANGE WHO WE ARE.

Can you imagine the pressure Daniel was under? If he gets this wrong, he, his friends, and even some people he probably didn't like very much would all be murdered because of the temper of a deranged king. There was no room for error here. Daniel not only handles the pressure in an incredible way, he also gives us a model for how we can do the same thing when the time comes.

First, Daniel shows us that we should never let the pressure of culture change who we are. The Babylonian goal was to completely replace the culture of their captives with their own. They sought to take away the things that unified the people of God, to erase the things that set them apart, and to make them forget that Babylon was not their home. They wanted to completely alter the identity of the captives. But Daniel wouldn't let that happen. I find it interesting that Daniel was only referred to as Belteshazzar three times in this book and each time it is accompanied by his true name. Daniel refused to conform to the Babylonian culture. He knew who he was, and he wasn't about to let an earthly king pressure him into abandoning his heavenly one. Like Daniel, we must refuse to let culture and the pressure it throws at us change who we are.

Daniel also shows us that we should prepare for big decisions before we need to make those big decisions. The Babylonian method of cultural destruction was not a new thing. It was a pretty common strategy for overtaking other lands. But scripture tells us that Daniel "had purposed in his heart not to defile himself with the king's food" (Dan. 1:8 NIV). We don't know when Daniel made this decision, but we do know that he made it prior to being seated at the king's table. We make too many life-altering decisions on the fly and honestly, it shows. Too many parents don't think about how they'll pass their faith onto their kids until they're headed off to college. Too many teenagers decide how they will respond to offers of alcohol or drugs the moment someone hands them the bottle, the joint, or the pills. Too many young people wait to decide their stance on sex before marriage until they are in the heat of the moment and their brain is full of chemicals that whisper, "this is the one." Too many business leaders decide how to handle money or company resources in the moments in which they are pressured to cut corners or fudge the numbers a little bit. And too many pastors, ministry leaders, and others in positions of authority decide on healthy boundaries only after they find themselves alone, exhausted, and incapable of making wise decisions.

In those moments, it's too late. These pressures, unchecked by established values, reduce our brains to the "if it feels good do it" level of reasoning and before we know it we've done something we can't take back. Daniel decided not to defile himself well before he smelled the bacon or tasted the wine. This type of pressure is defeated by defining your values and making the types of decisions in advance that point you toward becoming the person you are designed to become.

Daniel's story shows that when things get difficult, we should seek God and Godly community. When faced with an impossible situation, Daniel's first instinct was to pray and to invite his community to do the same. It was this commitment to prayer and community that ultimately led to his rescue and the rescue of his friends. Never underestimate what can happen when God's people gather in prayer.

Daniel also never forgot who the star of the show was. When the king's magicians declare that no man can do what the king is demanding Daniel doesn't contradict that, he actually agrees. He then declares that instead there is a God in heaven who can and will reveal such things. Daniel directs attention towards God, never towards himself. He knew that it was God's power at work that allowed him to reveal and interpret the dream. Alone, Daniel knew he was as good as dead. But thanks to God's power and His intervention, Daniel and his friends could have life. When you are able to walk through pressure, never forget who got you through to the other side. Alone, we don't have what it takes to stand strong. But as we discussed in chapter four, when we release the things we have to God and allow Him to use it, we are able to accomplish incredible things.

Finally, not only did Daniel successfully reveal and interpret the dream, he helped King Nebuchadnezzar recognize God's power which led to a major cultural shift. Nebuchadnezzar declared in front of his officials and wise men that "Surely [Daniel's] God is the God of gods and the Lord of kings and a revealer of mysteries, for you were able to reveal this mystery" (Dan. 2:47 NIV). Daniel's ability to handle this life-threatening pressure brought knowledge of God to a pagan nation.

Eventually a new King would come to power and Daniel would face this level of pressure again. Just like before, he would lean on his values and his trust in God to get him through that difficult time as well. Daniel's decisions equipped him for a lifetime of being able to thrive under pressure. What pressures are you facing that are threatening to derail you?

Looking back on my own struggles, it was through sharing my feelings and burdens with some close friends and family members that I was able to begin dismantling the negative thoughts and manufactured expectations that were causing me to feel such pressure. Thanks to my community, I was able to process and release the pressure that was building up all while clinging to the truth of who I was and who God had called me to be. Just like that tiny piece of plastic in a coffee bag, I was able to release the negative things that threatened to cause an explosion and to cling to the true things that mattered and that were shaping me to be more like Christ and pointing me toward His plan for my life.

While I am far from having this all figured out, I can at least confidently say that these days, Luisa is no longer my spirit animal. If I had to pick one, it would probably be something like a moose. Not sure why, just the first thing that came to mind. However, Luisa and her awesome theme song helped me to identify and address something in my life that was just beneath the surface threatening to explode. Let me encourage you to ask yourself, what's hiding out beneath the surface that you need to address? What decisions do you need to make now to protect your future? What values do you need to establish to help you navigate pressure in the right way and guide your decision-making process? Daniel got this right and if we follow his example, we can too. Don't let pressure derail you. Instead, recognize it as part of the process and create healthy rhythms and relationships that can serve as outlets when it does creep in. As we'll discuss in the next chapter, these high pressure, high stakes experiences may be preparing you with the exact tools you need.

CHAPTER SEVEN

THE GRIND

"KEEP YOUR DREAMS BIG AND YOUR STEPS SMALL."

—BRAD TATE

Our coffee journey is getting close to the end as our beans are now in a bag and ready for use. We'll skip the part about going to the store and purchasing the beans because well, hopefully you understand that part of the process and, if you're anything like me, you believe that grocery stores are the worst, and shopping in one can only crush your dreams, not support them. Harsh? Yes. Accurate? Probably not, but that's where I'm at right now. I do not like grocery stores. No, I'm not going to explain why and I don't really know why you brought it up. Let's move on.

The next step in the process of enjoying a delicious cup of coffee is to grind the beans. Maybe you buy your beans ground and you've never thought about this, but it is actually a crucial step. If you don't grind the beans, they won't extract and you don't have coffee, you have bean soup, but with really crunchy beans. Maybe a hot cereal kind of situation. Which begs the question is cereal also soup? Of course, it is, but that's not what we're here to discuss. Back to the grind. At this point, you probably know where this is going. But don't skip this one, this is not the "put your head down, keep doing the same thing over and over, and grind it out" kind of grinding.

THE WAY YOU NAVIGATE TODAY, HAS THE ABILITY
TO AFFECT WHAT YOU CAN DO IN THE FUTURE.

At the risk of giving away the next chapter, there are endless ways to brew coffee but those options become limited based on how you grind it. Some brew methods, like a French press, require a coarse grind, and some, like a drip brewer or pour over, require a finer grind. If you grind something too fine for a particular method, you end up with grounds in your cup. If you grind something too coarse for a particular method, extraction doesn't happen, and you get some weak watered-down version of coffee and that is just... wrong on many levels. What does this have to do with becoming who you were created to be? Everything. The way you walk through this step will either support or limit the next one. The way you navigate today, has the ability to affect what you can do in the future.

If a coffee bean were alive, I imagine it would say that grinding is the most painful part of the process. I'd like to think I understand. Sometimes we feel like life is a grinder. We're pressed, crushed, chopped up into little pieces, and eventually thrown into boiling hot water so that all of the best parts of us can be extracted out and what remains can be tossed aside. Wow, that metaphor got a little dark and way too real. So, how can we take something that is painful and use it to help ourselves move forward and become the very best possible version of who we are created to be? The simple answer is that we celebrate our experiences, our stories, our past, and even our pain in a way that allows it to shape and prepare us for the future.

As I think about the concept of this grinding, I think back to my early ministry years. I had been a youth pastor for about five years when I experienced what felt like a major roadblock. I felt like I was stuck with no visible path forward. I was serving at a campus of a large multi-site church, and I had just watched my first class of seniors graduate. This was the first class of students I had been ministering to since they were in sixth grade. It felt like the end of an era, and I was very confused as to what I should do next. Through prayer and several conversations with people in leadership, I believed God was preparing me to take a next step, but I couldn't figure out what that step was. After more prayer, seeking more counsel, and thinking through a long list of possibilities, I decided I wanted to move into a college and young adult ministry role. I shared these desires with several leaders at my church and things started to move forward. After coming to the conclusion that it was time for a change, we began to discuss some possibilities. That's when, fairly suddenly, things went in a drastically different direction. Before I knew it, I was in a role where I was responsible for creating video content and leading fourth and fifth grade students.

To me, this felt like a major left turn. Over the next seven years I felt adrift, bouncing around within the church through a long list of different roles. I was a worship leader, a tech director, an online pastor, a creative pastor, a leadership development pastor, and somewhere in all of that I went full time at Starbucks and became a store manager. Every time I made a move, I felt like I had finally found the thing I was searching for. I believed with each shift I had finally answered the question of "what's next?" But eventually, every one of these moves would end with what felt like a giant door being slammed in my face. I remember experiencing some of the lowest lows of my life and a nonstop sense of questioning my identity during this season. Over those years I experienced some major ministry wins and yet, I still felt empty, directionless, and purposeless. I knew I was learning skills and valuable lessons but none of them felt like they mattered. None of it seemed to have a point. It was a painful season of asking God if He was done with me while desperately holding on to the hope that there was something more.

As I look back on this season it brings to mind the story of a guy named Joseph. In Genesis 37 we zoom in on his story. Joseph was one of 12 sons of Jacob, who by this point had been renamed Israel and was to be a patriarch from whom God's chosen people would begin to grow. Joseph was the quintessential "golden child" and his dad's unquestioned favorite among the brothers. His dad regularly showered him with gifts, the finest of which was an extremely lavish and expensive coat that made his brothers jealous and bitter towards him. Joseph was somewhat of a dreamer and was always very quick to share those dreams with his brothers. Unfortunately for Joseph, those dreams often cast him in a ruling role over the rest of the family relegating them to be his subjects and servants. The major issue with this was that 10 of Joseph's brothers were older than him. In the culture of that day, every one of them would have to die before Joseph could rise to such a position in the family.

Things get pretty intense one day and Joseph's brothers decide to kill him. However, before they carry out their plan, cooler heads prevail and instead of killing him, they decide to sell him to a passing caravan of slave traders (side note: if you are part of a group where the "cooler heads" option is slavery over murder, find a new group). The traders travel to Egypt where they sell Joseph to a man named Potiphar. Despite his situation, Joseph honors Potiphar and works hard. Eventually Joseph finds favor in Potiphar's eyes and because of his stellar character and work ethic, Joseph is put in charge of Potiphar's estate. Under Joseph's leadership and care, the only things Potiphar has to concern himself with is when to eat and sleep. Things are going well for Joseph until Potiphar's wife catches feelings and decides she wants Joseph to sleep with her. Joseph repeatedly denies these advances and continues to work with excellence. One day Potiphar's wife grabs Joseph by the cloak and demands he sleep with her. Joseph basically shakes off the cloak and runs from the house leaving the garment behind. Potiphar's wife, now holding a "smoking gun," abuses her position of power, accuses Joseph of attempted rape and Potiphar has Joseph thrown in prison. All of a sudden, Joseph's hard work and the trust he had gained is reduced to the sound of a cell door slamming shut.

Let's recap: Joseph went from being dad's favorite to being sold into slavery by his own family. Then, from becoming Potiphar's favorite to being falsely accused (because Joseph was also kinda Potiphar's wife's favorite), and finally imprisoned. However, Joseph doesn't quit being who he is. Joseph continues to work with excellence and eventually, he rises through the ranks of the prison landing himself in charge once again. Scripture tells us that "the keeper of the prison paid no attention to anything that was in Joseph's charge" (Gen. 39:23 NIV) This could have been the part where Joseph attempts to make a daring escape and return triumphantly to his father. But that's not how the story goes. Instead, Joseph continues to work hard and trust God through the grinding. Eventually Joseph meets two formerly influential prisoners who have committed some sort of offense against the King of Egypt. One night they each have a pretty unsettling dream. They share their dreams with Joseph and ask him what they mean. Joseph, through the Lord's empowerment, is able to interpret these dreams right away. To one prisoner, the king's cupbearer, Joseph says, "Good news! You're out of here in a few days and you'll be right back to your former place in the king's service. Hey, don't forget about me when you're there. Can you let the king know that I was falsely imprisoned and if he's not too busy, it'd be really cool if he'd come get me out of here?" The cupbearer says, "sure thing Joseph. You'll be out of here before you know it." The other prisoner's news was unfortunately not so uplifting. To the king's baker, Joseph said, "You're not going to make it out of here alive. Unfortunately, the king is going to have you executed."

As Joseph predicted, the King restored the cupbearer to his former position, and all was well for him. However, in all of the excitement – and probably paperwork – of his rehire, the cupbearer completely forgets about Joseph.

It wasn't until two years later that Joseph's story finally began to change. One night, the king himself has an unsettling dream, and he shares it with the cupbearer. The cupbearer tells the king something to the effect of, "We should call my dreams guy. He'll help you out." The king says, "Where do we find him?" The cupbearer responds, "Oh yeah, he's in prison. I was going to tell you about him like two years ago but now's probably good. I mean, it's not like he was going anywhere."

The King calls for Joseph who of course is able to interpret the dream. Joseph reveals that Egypt will experience seven years of abundance followed by seven years of terrible famine. The King, recognizing

Joseph's wisdom, seeks his advice on what to do. After Joseph lays out an awesome plan, the king looks to him and says, "Great. You're in charge. Make it happen." Joseph begins to execute his plan and is eventually put in charge to the point where all the king has to worry about is when to eat and when to sleep.

Joseph's plan is such a success that when the famine spreads to the neighboring lands people travel to Egypt to buy food. Guess who happens to show up in Egypt looking for food: Joseph's brothers. As they bow before him, Joseph realizes that his original dream has come true. Finally, Joseph has the opportunity to lord it over them and have his "gotcha" moment. Instead, he recognizes that even though his brothers meant to harm him, God used the painful grinding season for the good of an entire nation and the good of Joseph's own family as well. Joseph's faithfulness through his suffering eventually led to the rescue of his family and the Israelite people as a whole.

This story covers about 12 pages in the Bible. You can read all of it in around 30 minutes, but Joseph's story actually took place over the course of about twenty years. From the time Joseph shared his "impossible" dream with his brothers to the time he rescued them from starvation was two entire decades. I don't know about you but when things get hard, I'm way less like Joseph and way more like Kevin in the CPR training scene of The Office. I'm often thinking, "I can't keep doing this forever" and God has to remind me that "it has literally been twenty seconds." I can't imagine living through twenty years of pain, captivity, and abuse.

Throughout this story Joseph was constantly being put through the wringer. Sold by his family, living as a slave, eventually beginning to see some good in all of it, only to be falsely imprisoned, forgotten, betrayed, left behind, and finally put into a position in which he could make a difference. It would have been easy for Joseph to see his life as ruined from the moment those slave traders bought him. But he didn't. Joseph knew what God had promised him. Joseph knew that his time would come. Joseph knew that the God who gave him the dream is a good God who loved and had a plan to use his life in a big way. Joseph used this knowledge to give him peace in that process. He never rejected the trials that were in front of him. He never tried to run away, manipulate the situation, or push his way to the front of the line. We do not even see him resentful at his circumstances. Instead, he stayed faithful in the process knowing that God was at work in his situation. He knew that his situation wasn't a diversion from his dream but it was preparation for his dream. Every time his story took a negative turn (which was all of them. All the turns), Joseph remained faithful. And it was that faithfulness that projected him forward. What if every time we experienced pain, a setback, a problem, or a roadblock, we saw it as preparation for what's to come? What if we reframed the grinding that life seems so excited to put us through and saw it as preparation for something amazing?

For me, this grinding took place over seven years. In that time, I was never sold into slavery, falsely imprisoned, or left to rot in a cell. However, I did experience what it was like to have my dreams ripped away. I did understand the feelings of being helpless. I knew what it was like to be so sure about something only to have a door slammed in my face. There were many days where I felt alone, forgotten, and abandoned. There were even times where I thought I saw a light at the end of the tunnel only to have that light put out just before I could reach it. There were times I wanted to give up, times I wanted to walk away, and times when I wanted to scream at God and ask Him why He gave me these dreams only to have them constantly dangle just out of reach. That season was confusing and dark. It was seven years of wandering and longing and questioning who I was. But, Like Joseph, it was also seven years of growing and preparing and discovering answers to my identity questions.

I didn't see that what felt like aimless wandering was an extremely purposeful pathway that God was laying out before me. At every step of the journey, I was learning new skills, adding new tools, and building new relationships that were giving me the strength I needed for the present and shaping me for the future.

As I write this today, I serve my church as the NextGen pastor. In this role I oversee all ministries from birth through graduating seniors. Here are some of the skills you need to have at least some familiarity with to do this job: Leadership development, how the creative process works, how to minister online, how to lead and communicate with high schoolers, middle schoolers, and younger kids. You even need to know at least a little bit about running a business.

EVERY EXPERIENCE, EVERY RELATIONSHIP,
EVERY SKILL, AND EVERY HURT HAS BEEN
PREPARING YOU TO DO THAT THING FOR WHICH
YOU WERE CREATED.

The years spent learning these skills were tough. Every turn felt like a distraction or a roadblock. Moving from middle and high school ministry to fourth and fifth graders felt like a major step backward, but I learned patience in that season and how to communicate to a different audience. Shifting into full time creative arts felt like a step outside of my calling but it was there that I learned to think differently, try new things, and truly shape culture. Leaving the church to go make coffee felt like giving up and leaving my dreams of being a pastor behind. But it was in that coffee shop that I learned to lead people and develop those under my leadership. Every step of the way God's hand was guiding, teaching, and refining me. What felt to me like a series of roadblocks, slammed doors, and getting my heart and soul ripped apart was actually preparing me for the seat in which I now sit. Truly, I love what I get to do. I fully believe it is the best job in the world and I am so thankful that I was able to (sort of) faithfully walk through the process of the grinding to get here. I didn't always do it perfectly or gracefully. I didn't always handle the grinding well in the moment. But thanks to God's grace, I made it through, and I didn't quit.

The grinding can be painful. Scratch that. The grinding is painful. It usually feels destructive and counterproductive. But if we are willing to recognize it as preparation we, like Joseph, may find ourselves in the position to make a big difference for our families and in the world. We just might look back and be able to see how our grinding was purposeful from the start. If you are in a season of grinding, have the courage and strength to trust God in the process. If you're reading this book while drinking a cup of coffee, you must understand that the beans that make up that cup were planted at least four years ago. It takes a minimum of four years to make that drink. If it takes that long to make a simple cup of coffee, how much more should we be willing to prepare ourselves to live out our purpose according to God's timeline? Your life has a purpose and you have been preparing for it since day one. Every experience, every relationship, every skill, and every hurt has been preparing you to do that thing for which you were created. The choice comes down to this: will you push through the hard stuff to find the reward on the other side, or will you fold? I believe you have what it takes to see this thing through. Don't give up, get ready. Don't fold, fight. Don't walk away, instead run toward the peace that Jesus brings. Let Him guide you on the path that he's laid for you knowing that every step, every day, and every experience matters. They are all preparing you to do the great works that He has prepared for you long ago. Trust the process, walk through the hard stuff, then get out there and crush it!

CHAPTER EIGHT

BREWING, WHAT TO DO WHEN THE OPTIONS ARE SO LIMITED
*A NOT-SO-SUBTLE LESSON IN SARCASM

"WHEN YOU COME TO A FORK IN THE ROAD, TAKE IT."

—YOGI BERA

Deciding how to brew coffee is like a five-year-old deciding what they want to be when they grow up. Endless possibilities exist. Firefighter, doctor, lawyer, fashion designer, mechanic, forest pathologist; and those are just the ones I heard from my oldest daughter when she was five. To be fair, she didn't say forest pathologist, she said "tree doctor" but I figured I'd use the correct term so I wouldn't have to explain what "tree doctor" meant. Except I ended up explaining it and that's kind of like throwing two stones at one bird. Let's just accept that she is a genius and get back on track.

If you're the type to overthink any decision you ever have to make (like whether to explain "tree doctor" for example), brewing coffee could be overwhelming. I would be willing to bet if you went on Twitter and asked everyone for their preferred method, you would get dozens of responses, each not only telling you the "proper way" but also unpacking all the reasons that every other method is incorrect, ridiculous, and doesn't respect the integrity or inherent flavor of the bean. In fact, I asked my social media community what the best way to brew coffee was and why and I got this answer within seconds: "Espresso 18 grams in 36out with Colombian Lucy. Aim for a 26 sec shot and 11 sec preinfusion. It's better than everyone else because I'm the first to comment and because it's a process that is very satisfying when you get it right." I worked at Starbucks for almost 5 years and have no idea what most of those words even mean! My favorite answer has to be: "I usually make a Keurig while waiting for a pot to brew. I've tried IV, but the hot coffee melts the tubing." If you've never felt this way, I'm surprised you are holding this book. Don't get me wrong, I still glad you're here.

When it comes to brewing coffee, there are just way too many options. Drip brew, cold brew, espresso, percolator, Keurig (which hurts my heart to even type) moka pots, Chemex, French press, Turkish, cupping, pour over, aero press, that thing Walter White's other assistant did in Breaking Bad, and apparently even something called a Seven and Me. And now that your internal voice sounds like Forrest Gump talking about the many ways to cook shrimp, I rest my case. There are so many options and the right one ultimately comes down to one simple variable: what you like. The right way to brew coffee is however you want to brew it that day.

Personally, I use a drip brewer when I want hot coffee, cold brew when I want iced coffee, and an aero press sporadically when I decide I want to be an aero press guy again. At the end (or more likely the beginning) of the day, it's up to you. I used to work with a guy who loved to brew with a Chemex and on multiple occasions declared that it was the only way to brew. Because he had a respectable beard and spoke about it with such conviction, I began to believe him. One day he hatched a plan to get everyone in the office to go in together and purchase an office Chemex along with all the other supplies and accessories we would need. I don't remember the exact number of dollars it was going to cost each of us but because of the price tag, most of my coworkers were out before he could say "goose neck kettle." And thus, we didn't get the Chemex. As I look back on that story, I realize, the only reason I wanted the Chemex was because he had such conviction and had positioned himself as the premier coffee brewing authority of the great state of our office. I didn't want the Chemex, I wanted to be accepted as a fellow coffee connoisseur.

I don't know about you, but I get caught in the comparison trap a lot. When I see someone who is doing something that I think I should be doing, I immediately go all in on that thing. That day I wanted to be a "Chemex guy" because my office mate was a Chemex guy. Because of the comparison trap I have been a designer jeans guy, a boots guy (cowboy, Chelsea, chukka, etc.), a guitar pedal guy, a video games guy, a car guy, and now a sneaker guy. While comparison didn't initially pull me into any of these hobbies, it has been a major driving force in just how "in" I am in each.

Let me give you a recent example. As I mentioned earlier, I am a musician and I love playing guitar. I also just love guitars in general. The look, the feel, the sounds they make, the craftsmanship, the list goes on. All of these things make the actual guitar just as much a piece of art as any of the sounds that could come out of it. There is something special about seeing a brand-new guitar or a really old guitar hanging on a wall surrounded by a bunch of other new or old guitars. For a long time, I would buy and sell guitars as a side hustle and eventually found myself with three guitars that I really liked. I had those three guitars for a couple of years when the unthinkable happened: one of my friends had the audacity, the nerve – nay, the unmitigated gall – to get a new acoustic guitar. She didn't even have the courtesy to warn me! As soon as it happened, the comparison trap launched full force in the back of my mind. Her new guitar was perfect in every way. It was a great size, really easy to play, had a great sound and was just all around better (in my head) than my vintage 1986 Guild D-25. All of a sudden, I wanted, no, I needed a new guitar. I had to have it. I had to keep up. And so, I did what I do in such a dire situation and started searching the Facebook marketplace for the perfect guitar. Unfortunately, the Facebook marketplace let me down by being fresh out of the exact guitar I wanted for less than forty dollars. Additionally, the "stuff Brandon wants" line in our budget was not healthy enough even if I had found that guitar for less than forty dollars.

So instead of getting a new guitar, I suffered in silent jealousy for quite some time. I said things like "I love this for you," and "I am so glad you were able to get this beautiful new guitar that you needed to do your job as a professional musician." But on the inside, the comparison trap had me spinning out of control. Well, as it happened, I was getting ready to graduate from my bachelor's program and my wife asked me if there was anything I'd like as a graduation gift. My hasty answer was a new guitar. So, right after graduation, I received money from several family members and started looking for a new guitar. After doing extensive research for nearly an hour and playing every guitar I could get my hands on inside of one Guitar Center I made my decision. Coincidentally, the decision I made was to get the same model guitar that my friend had purchased in a slightly different finish. Shocker.

Well, a few months later her guitar experienced what I would define as rapid unscheduled disassembly. The bridge came off of the body and the cost to fix it was going to be way higher than the original value of the guitar. I was sad for her, but I still really liked mine and for a brief moment, felt like I was ahead on points (I know, I am a monster.) It was a great sounding guitar... until it wasn't. One day it started buzzing really bad and I noticed that the bridge was starting to separate from the body. At that point it was a ticking time bomb and only a matter of time before it would experience the same catastrophic failure as hers. For months it hung on my wall as a silent reminder that comparison can steal your time, your joy, and your sweet, sweet, graduation money. Thankfully, before it exploded, I was able to sell it to a luthier (a craftsperson who builds or repairs guitars and other stringed instruments) who could fix it and flip it. Unfortunately, I had to sell it for way less than it cost me. My college graduation present was gone and eventually, thanks to a good day on the SNKRS app, became a pair of Fire Red Air Jordan 3's. They don't sound nearly as good as the guitar did, but they can really tie a fit together.

The comparison trap ended up costing me what should have been a really meaningful gift. If I wasn't so caught up in what I didn't have, I could have focused on what I did have. I already had, and still have, a great guitar that will probably outlive us all! I didn't need another one. What I needed, and still need on a regular basis, is a sharper focus on contentment. As you are pursuing your dreams and your calling, don't focus on someone else's. Stay focused on yours. The writer of Hebrews offers great encouragement in chapters eleven and twelve. He tells us that faith is "confidence in what we hope for and assurance about what we do not see" (Heb. 11:1 NIV). Throughout the chapter the writer paints a portrait of faith, citing heroes of the Bible. Each of these heroes is a testimony of what it means to live out your own path, your own calling, and your own story. They are great examples of what it means to live a life focused on kingdom purpose. As we flip the page to chapter 12 the author begins by saying "Therefore." As a side note, I learned in Bible college and from my boss, that anytime you see a "therefore" you should ask what the therefore is there for. In this context, "therefore" means "because of what I just told you…." The writer is saying, "Because I just gave you all of these examples of faith and how they lived it out, you should pay close attention to this next part." He goes on to say, "since we are surrounded by such a great cloud of witnesses, let us throw off everything that hinders and the sin that so easily entangles. And let us run with perseverance the race marked out for us, fixing our eyes on Jesus, the pioneer and perfecter of faith" (Heb. 12:1 NIV).

The author of Hebrews tells us a couple of things here that are so important if we want to live the life we were created to live. First, as believers, we have a massive crowd cheering us on. We are surrounded by a great cloud of witnesses, those heroes of the faith, who are constantly right there in the stands rooting for us. So, when the road gets rough and you feel alone, remember our heroes are cheering us on.

COMPARISON ROBS US OF OUR CREATIVITY
AND STEALS OUR JOY.

Second, he says to throw off everything that hinders and the sin that so easily entangles. What's important here is to notice that not everything that hinders us is sin. We can be hindered by good things that aren't the right things. We can be hindered by a desire to please everyone. We can be hindered by overcommitting ourselves to the wrong things. There are plenty of hindrances that aren't sinful. But if we are going to live out our unique calling, we have to be willing to consider whether some good things have become hindrances.

Next, the author addresses the sin that so easily entangles. If you are weighed down by sin, hand it over to Jesus. If you are struggling with sin of any kind, find safe people who you can lean on for prayer and accountability. Don't let sin steal your calling. Allow Jesus to do what He came to do through the finished work of the cross and let Him make you new.

Finally, run your race. The encouragement here is to run the race that is marked out for YOU. Not for your neighbor, not for the pastor or business leader down the street, not your old friends from high school, not your friend who just bought a new thing that you now have to have, but instead, run the race that is marked out for you. Comparison robs us of our creativity and steals our joy. If we get caught up trying to be someone else, who will fill the unique role that you are destined to fill? You have a unique mark to make on the world, a gift worth giving, and a story worth sharing. Run your own race.

The Apostle Paul understood this more than anyone. He was a Pharisee but eventually, an encounter with Jesus changed the course of his entire life. God called him to go and preach the Gospel throughout the world but specifically to the gentiles. At this point there are a few things working against Paul. First, initially no one trusted that he had actually changed his life. Paul had given believers plenty of reason to be skeptical of this life change and to be fearful of him and his motives. Second, even when he did become an apostle of Jesus, he was kind of viewed as an outsider among the group. He and Peter seemed to have a tumultuous relationship at best. Finally, Paul was viewed as a traitor among the Pharisees and Jewish community at large. There were many attempts made on Paul's life throughout his story and eventually, he would be martyred by the Romans.

Outside of these relational challenges, Paul suffered many physical hardships and setbacks. In Second Corinthians 11, Paul gives us a rundown of some of these challenges. He says:

Five times I received from the Jews the forty lashes minus one. Three times I was beaten with rods, once I was pelted with stones, three times I was shipwrecked, I spent a night and a day in the open sea, I have been constantly on the move. I have been in danger from rivers, in danger from bandits, in danger from my fellow Jews, in danger from Gentiles; in danger in the city, in danger in the country, in danger at sea; and in danger from false believers. I have labored and toiled and have often gone without sleep; I have known hunger and thirst and have often gone without food; I have been cold and naked. (2 Cor 11:24-27 NIV)

In all of this, it would have been easy to give up and walk away. It would have been even easier to compare his life to that of the other apostles and get bitter. Paul could easily have prayed, "Lord, it sure would be nice if for once Peter could get shipwrecked instead of me. That guy could use some time on an island with his thoughts!" But this was not Paul's character. Paul was a man who was focused on his calling, his work, and his race. He knew that anything worth doing would require him to do the hard work and avoid comparing himself to others. Paul's laser focus on his own race and his own unique calling from God led him to evangelize, plant countless churches, and pen over two thirds of the New Testament. Paul became one of the most impactful people in all of history and he did so because he simply ran his race. Christians today know Jesus better because Paul ran his race.

In one of his final letters before he was martyred, Paul writes to Timothy, his young protege and says,

In the presence of God and of Christ Jesus, who will judge the living and the dead, and in view of his appearing and his kingdom, I give you this charge: Preach the word; be prepared in season and out of season; correct, rebuke, and encourage—

with great patience and careful instruction. For the time will come when people will not put up with sound doctrine. Instead, to suit their own desires, they will gather around them a great number of teachers to say what their itching ears want to hear. They will turn their ears away from the truth and turn aside to myths. But you, keep your head in all situations, endure hardship, do the work of an evangelist, discharge all the duties of your ministry. For I am already being poured out like a drink offering, and the time for my departure is near. I have fought the good fight, I have finished the race, I have kept the faith. Now there is in store for me the crown of righteousness, which the Lord, the righteous Judge, will award to me on that day— and not only to me, but also to all who have longed for his appearing. (2 Tim. 4:1-8 NIV)

Did you see it? Paul encourages his young friend Timothy to run the race. Don't get distracted by the people who tell you that you're not good enough. Don't buckle to the pressure of the world and its broken messages. Don't give up when people reject you and the truth that you hold. But run your race. At this point in the letter, Paul shifts gears and reflects back on his own race. He knew that his time on earth was coming to an end. He tells Timothy, "I did this. I ran my race. I fought the good fight and now, I am going to receive my prize."

Running your own race looks a lot like brewing coffee the way you like it. Recently, I found myself in a conversation with a friend about coffee brew methods. He began to list all of the coffee equipment he owns. The list was extensive and included one method that ended with the word sock. That sounds gross. Near the end of the conversation, I asked him how often he used each of the items on his list. I was not surprised when he told me that he uses most of these items rarely or never. He had two or three that he used regularly and another for when company was over, and he needed a larger quantity. Otherwise, the items in his collection mostly occupied space and saw little use. Most of his collection was purchased because someone at some point convinced him that he needed some different, new, or exciting piece of coffee gear to keep up with the trends and maintain his status as the top coffee guy within his sphere of influence.

Does this sound familiar? Maybe it's not coffee gear for you. Comparison can sneak in anywhere. Comparison says, "I can't believe you're still using a drip brewer. What year is it? Do you ride a horse to work too? Haven't you heard of the old dirty sock method?" When it comes to running our own race, it sounds more like, "I can't believe you are still working that job when you could be an influencer selling makeup made from the tears of Scandinavian unicorns to all of your friends." We may think the race we are running doesn't matter or that it's too mundane. But at the end of the day, it is all about being who God created you to be. It all comes down to taking the steps that God has set before you, not before someone else.

AT THE END OF THE DAY, IT IS ALL ABOUT BEING
WHO GOD CREATED YOU TO BE.

What could God do with your life if you got serious about running your own race? What could you accomplish as it relates to your dreams, your goals, and His kingdom? How much more time could you spend with your family if you avoid chasing the status and lifestyle of someone else's. How much more joy could you have at work if you weren't silently competing with the person in the next office? How much financial freedom could you have if you weren't striving to keep up with the Joneses. Comparing yourself to someone else will never help you. It is a weight and a hindrance. It slows us down, steals our joy, and halts our momentum. That's why racehorses wear blinders. Yes, comparison even affects the animal kingdom. Don't let comparison steal your joy and your purpose. Run your race. The greatest prize is at the finish line.

CHAPTER NINE

TIMING IS EVERYTHING; THE TRAGIC DEATH OF AN ESPRESSO SHOT

"THE SECRET TO LIFE IS TIMING. "

—JEREMY IRONS

One of the greatest lessons I have ever learned from my good friend, the coffee bean, came very early in my coffee journey. As a new employee at Starbucks, you go through some fairly extensive training. Over the first two weeks as a barista, you spend most of your time at a table learning about the products and the processes. As a part of the training, new baristas taste almost every coffee and tea on the menu within their first 90 days of employment. This process provides the opportunity to sit with several managers, shift supervisors, and other baristas to do coffee and food tastings. It not only increases the product knowledge for the new barista, but it builds community among the team and can serve as a refresher for some of the seasoned vets who's training days are but a distant memory. On one such day, my store manager and I sat down to do a tasting of espresso. Brewing shots of espresso is slightly different from the other brew methods in that it is a bit more nuanced and temperamental. With espresso shots, everything matters; the coarseness of the beans, the temperature of the water, the time it takes to brew, every seemingly small detail counts.

Of all of these factors, one of the most important in a good shot of espresso is how long it sits between when you brew it and when you use it. On this day, the goal was to make the critical nature of this truth abundantly clear. When I tasted my first shot of espresso it was smooth, balanced, roasty, and sweet, and it looked beautiful sitting there in that small glass. The second shot was bitter and stale. It was even a bit sour and it looked nothing like the other one. Honestly, it was really gross. These two shots were brewed at the same time in the same machine. The only variable between the two was that I drank one of them first. What separated these two espresso shots was a mere 20 seconds.

I still wish I could have seen the face I made when I sipped that second shot. I wouldn't be surprised if it was similar to the "bitter-beer face" that Fosters Beer used in their advertising back in the 90's. That, or a face similar to the moment a young child discovers facial contortionism the first time they taste a lemon. I wasn't sure if I should thank my manager for fast-tracking my appreciation of the espresso process or punch her for subjecting me to such torture. I opted for the former instead of choosing violence. I'm still not sure I made the right choice. Thankfully, all of the baristas I would later sentence to the same fate over the course of my time as a trainer would make the same choice and channel their distaste into perfecting their craft, ensuring that they would never subject one of our beloved customers to a similar fate*.

The trick with espresso is that all you have to do to prevent it from dying and becoming this bitter, sour, discolored monstrosity is to add some milk or water to it. In essence, all you have to do is use it for its intended purpose within the right amount of time. By doing this, a small shot of espresso can become a delicious, handcrafted beverage and can make a huge impact on a person's day.

That simple tasting was the beginning of my love for espresso and all of its nuanced glory. I began to appreciate the process and the art of getting it just right, if for no other reason than to make sure I never had to taste a dead shot again. I would regularly time my shots, make adjustments, test the machine again, and make more adjustments. I became the guy everyone came to when things seemed off. I knew the inner workings of the espresso machine and learned how to coax perfection out of it. I continued to perfect my craft to the point where I sounded like the Chemex guy from the last chapter but with espresso. I wanted the perfect shot every time and I knew that the perfect shot of espresso began with the right beans and ended up as part of something magical.

It takes about 80 whole beans to make a shot of espresso. As we have already discussed, those beans have been grown, hand-picked, processed, and roasted just to get to this point. Once they get into the bean hopper, they still need to be ground just right in order to make a great shot. Too coarse and the water will pass through the grounds too quickly resulting in a shot that is thin, watery, and under-extracted. Too fine and the water takes too long to get through the grounds resulting in an over-extracted bitter shot.

The perfect shot takes about 19 seconds to pull. These result in a shot that is fully extracted and exquisitely flavorful with three visible parts in the glass. First is the head, a thick layer of crema – a foam-like layer – on top of the shot; then the body, the middle, waterier layer of the shot; and finally, the heart, the rich, dark, lower layer of the shot. Once the shot finishes brewing it is good for just about 10 seconds. Before those ten seconds are over the espresso needs to be put in milk or water or it will die. This isn't some metaphorical or hypothetical death. No, you can visibly see the shot changing from this beautifully layered shot into a dark and murky mess. The crema begins to disperse, and the heart of the shot literally collapses and mixes with the body. It's actually a very sad sight for those who know what they're looking at. However, if you get it into a latte, an Americano, or a cappuccino, it remains flavorful and delicious for quite some time.

Let's break down the math of all of this. If we look at the time from grind to cup, the lifespan of an espresso shot is a total of 30 seconds. About 20 of those seconds are in brewing, or, the preparation stage. The other 10 seconds are in completion or the usefulness stage. Beyond that it is either fulfilling its purpose or has missed its opportunity and thus become bitter and fruitless. Two-thirds of the life of a single shot of espresso is spent in preparation, preparation to be a part of something great. The next third can be spent in waiting, but if we miss the opportunity to make use of it, it withers and dies.

Perhaps this feels all too familiar to you. Maybe it feels like you missed your chance. Maybe it's a mistake you've made that you feel you can never recover from. Maybe you believe that you are too old to change course or chase your dreams. Maybe you believe you're stuck in a situation that you can't get out of. Sometimes these feelings result from unrecognized potential. Your boss overlooks the gifts and talents you have to offer or simply doesn't have anything more to offer you. Whatever our specific circumstances, it is easy to feel overlooked, abandoned, forgotten, or devalued. I spent many years in this place feeling like I was wasting away being stuck with so much to offer but with no outlet. As I look back now, I recognize that this may have been partially true in limited seasons but even in those seasons I was actually still in the preparation phase.

More often the reason we feel like we're withering and dying is because of our own failure to pursue the big dreams to which God has called us. We can fail in many ways just like the shot of espresso. Sometimes we fail to spend enough time in the preparation stage. We jump the gun and get ourselves into trouble. Look at the life of Joseph from Genesis 37 that we discussed in chapter seven. He had a dream. It was a dream that God gave him directly. In this dream Joseph saw his brothers' bundles of grain bowing down to his bundle. In a second dream Joseph saw the sun, moon, and eleven stars bowing down before him. Joseph knew how to interpret these dreams. Ultimately, it meant that he would be the head or leader of his family. But as Joseph was the second youngest of the family, this was quite a statement. For him to say that everyone in the family would bow down to him meant he would usurp the family tradition and take the place of his oldest brother Reuben, jumping past his other ten brothers as well. As we discussed, Joseph's brothers didn't take kindly to his suggestion that he would rule over the whole family. One day an opportunity arose. Joseph was bringing lunch to his brothers who were working out in the fields. They quickly plotted to kill him and make it look like he'd been attacked by a wild animal. However, cooler heads prevailed and instead they sold him to a passing slave trader. Upgrade?

As we have already seen, Joseph's dreams would eventually come true. However, had he spent a little more time in preparation before he announced his dream, he may have been met with a little less resistance.

On the other hand, sometimes we get scared and want to stay in the preparation stage for way too long, like Moses and the Israelites on their journey to the Promised Land. God Himself led them out of Egypt. He fed them with manna from heaven and quenched their thirst with water from rocks. He parted the Red Sea allowing safe passage and escape from the pursuing Egyptian army. However, when they were faced with the choice to either walk into their purpose and acquire the land God had promised them or stand paralyzed by fear just a river away, they opted to stay in the desert angry at God and longing to be back in slavery to the Egyptians. Fear had gripped them because they saw a challenge in front of them that destroyed their confidence and eroded their trust in God. Because they didn't go in at the proper time, they began to wither, lose heart, and eventually an entire generation of Israelites would die in a desert within view of the promised land of Canaan.

IF YOU LET FEAR GRIP YOU, IF YOU LET THE FEAR OF THE UNKNOWN CRIPPLE YOU AND FORCE YOU TO STAY ON THE WRONG SIDE OF THE PROMISED LAND, YOUR SOUL WILL BEGIN TO WITHER.

Enter Joshua. Joshua had learned and prepared under Moses paying close attention to the promises and laws of God. He had been characterized by courage and faithfulness and when Moses's generation died out, the people looked to Joshua to lead them. Look at the call that Joshua received from God in Joshua chapter 1.

After the death of Moses, the servant of the Lord, the Lord said to Joshua, son of Nun, Moses' aide: "Moses my servant is dead. Now then, you and all these people, get ready to cross the Jordan River into the land I am about to give to them—to the Israelites. I will give you every place where you set your foot, as I promised Moses. Your territory will extend from the desert to Lebanon, and from the great river, the Euphrates—all the Hittite country—to the Mediterranean Sea in the west. No one will be able to stand against you all the days of your life. As I was with Moses, so I will be with you; I will never leave you nor forsake you. Be strong and courageous, because you will lead these people to inherit the land, I swore to their ancestors to give them. "Be strong and very courageous. Be careful to obey all the law my servant Moses gave you; do not turn from it to the right or to the left, that you may be successful wherever you go. Keep this Book of the Law always on your lips; meditate on it day and night, so that you may be careful to do everything written in it. Then you will be prosperous and successful. Have I not commanded you? Be strong and courageous. Do not be afraid; do not be discouraged, for the Lord your God will be with you wherever you go." (Jos. 1:1-9 NIV)

Joshua is a great example of someone who chased his purpose. He spent the appropriate amount of time preparing and he was ready to dive in when the time came. Like Moses and Joshua, at some point in your life you are going to be faced with a choice: a choice to pursue greatness or be crippled by fear. I don't know what the practical ramifications of that choice will look like for you, but I can promise you this: If you let fear grip you, if you let the fear of the unknown cripple you and force you to stay on the wrong side of the promised land, your soul will begin to wither. You will wonder what could have been had you just trusted God and dove into His calling. However, if you will do what Joshua did, if you will be strong and courageous, God will bless you. He will go before you, and He will be your rear guard. He will level the paths in front of you and, as He promised Joshua, everywhere you set foot will be on land that He has given you.

This type of trust in God does not mean there won't be challenges. In order to inhabit the Promised Land, Joshua and his army had to defeat 31 kings. They had to trust and follow God. They had to hold each other accountable and learn to discern God's will from their own desires. As Joshua and the Israelites pursued this promise, they experienced the joy of victory but at times they experienced crushing defeat. In the victories they learned that they could trust the Lord to go before and fight on their behalf. And in the defeat, they learned to lean into the Lord and let Him lead them forward instead of trying to fight the battles on their own.

None of this happened overnight. Like our delicious shot of espresso, there was a process through which Joshua prepared for what was ahead. He was willing to serve as Moses' aide for years and learn what it took to lead his people. He was willing to wait patiently and allow God to develop him through the process. And when the time came, he was ready to step into his calling and fulfill his God-given purpose. Joshua got the timing right and, despite the challenges before him, he was able to rise up and secure a home for Israel.

As we seek to fulfill our dreams and purpose, we will face similar challenges. But it is these challenges that strengthen our faith and build our character, providing us the tools we need to walk in everything He has called us to. Some of us have kings in our lives that we just can't seem to defeat, and those kings are currently standing on our land. They have occupied what God has promised us and too often we opt to sit in the corner and complain instead of fight. We need to take back our land. We need to look at our lives and realize that now is our time. Now is the time to fight for our land. The land of our family, the land of our marriages, of our friendships, our careers, our ministries, and our dreams. What kings are standing on your land? It's time to face them down and drive them out. We need to face down the kings of fear, pride, self-pity, unfaithfulness, greed, envy, or whatever king has cut you off at the knees. We have what these kings don't have and that is a purpose, a calling, and a passion directly given to us by God. It's time to be a Joshua generation, a generation that decides to go in and fight for what's ours.

Accept the calling that Joshua accepted and charge into your land with the confidence that God Himself has already given it to you. You have what it takes, you were made for this. Stand firm in that calling. Be strong and courageous and know that while we may face many kings, we are always backed by The King. He's the one that made it all, He rules over it all, and He is above it all. Don't let your life or your dreams wither and die. Our time is limited, don't waste it!

**I worked for a different coffee shop prior to learning this lesson and would often let espresso shots sit on the bar until I needed it to make a drink. If you ever purchased one of these drinks from me, I am sorry. I had no idea the true power which rested in my hands. I promise I'm not a monster!*

CHAPTER TEN

THE FIRST SIP AND THE FORGOTTEN CUP

"TO ME, THE SMELL OF FRESH-MADE COFFEE IS ONE OF THE GREATEST INVENTIONS."

—HUGH JACKMAN

Finally, we've come to the moment we've been waiting for, that glorious first sip. If you are reading this with a cup of coffee, as you should be, take a moment to think of how far these tiny beans have traveled and the process they've been through. Think of the pain they have endured. Think of the time they have spent in preparation so that they could make your morning a little bit better. They've been planted and taken years to go from seedling to tree and eventually to a coffee cherry. They have been harvested, probably by hand, through painstaking labor carried out on difficult terrain. They have been processed so that they can become a usable bean separated from the excess and prepared for use. They have been roasted, enduring the heat from the flames and the stress that caused them to crack, and cook, and expel the excess sugars and compounds that have no place in your perfect cup. They have been ground, being crushed, mashed, and ripped apart so that their flavors can be extracted into the waiting water. Finally, they have been brewed, releasing their flavors into your pot so that they could ultimately be poured out into your cup all to transform you from a lifeless zombie into a functional human adult.

As that first sip approaches, you take the carafe, hold it over your favorite mug, and listen to the sound as the hot liquid fills the empty cup. This is actually one of my favorite sounds that exists. You breathe in the aroma and allow the scent to fill your olfactory receptors giving you a preview of the amazing flavors to come. You watch the steam rise from the surface filling the air with the light vapor that assures you that warmth and comfort are on the way. You pour a splash of cream and watch it combine with the dark coffee mixing together into a beautiful swirling pattern as the two liquids become one. Finally, you lift the mug to your lips, tip it back, and take that highly anticipated first sip. The coffee washes over your palate, awakening your senses and giving you that morning pick-me-up that you've been anticipating since you laid your head on the pillow the night before. What a moment. What a culmination. It's taken literal years for those beans to get to this cup and finally, it's time to enjoy the payoff. What an experience, what a story. But at the end of the day, they are coffee beans, it's just what they do. Unless it isn't.

I got a new coffee maker for Christmas. It's amazing. The best thing about it is that I can program it to have the coffee ready when I wake up. Is this a modern miracle of science? No. Plenty of people have had access to this technology for years but for me, this is a new convenience. It's one of those situations where I had no idea I needed something so much and now that I have it, I can never go back. I can't go back to weighing out my beans while my eyes are still closed. I can't go back to measuring water in the dark because I don't want to wake anyone up. Nope, from this point forward, that stuff gets done in the nighttime. Now all I need to do is focus on not missing the cup when I make that first pour. It can be touch and go. Don't judge.

Another major benefit of this coffee maker is it has a larger capacity than my previous situation. For me, this means I make a pot of coffee and I just have it there available to me whenever I need another cup. My intake has gone from two cups in the morning to well... more. Much more. There is a downside to this and that is that some of that beautiful coffee tends to go to waste. Sometimes, this is because I simply don't finish the pot. Time slips away from me, I need to leave the house, and the rest of that coffee sits in the pot purposeless and forgotten. I blame my wife because she doesn't drink coffee and thus, won't contribute to eradicating this problem. As they say, no one's perfect. Barring this one obvious flaw, she might be as close as they come. But back to the topic at hand. Other times, I make myself a cup, set it down somewhere, and walk away. I move on to the next thing and completely forget I even made that cup of coffee. It's a real tragedy. In fact, the forgotten cup is the greatest tragedy in the coffee process. That statement may seem extreme but hear me out. Think again of what it takes, from planting to brewing, to get those beans into your cup. Yet they made it. They endured. They passed the quality checks and made it all the way to the end of the process and now they are on the precipice of living out their intended purpose. Instead, here they sit, forgotten on a counter, out of sight, out of mind, and slowly growing colder and becoming... a little gross.

Both for coffee and for us, distractions are the number one killer of purpose. It happens all the time. I have heard story after story of people who started down a path confident and assured that they were pursuing what God had for them, only to look up years down the road and find that distractions knocked them off course and sent them to a place they never intended to be. I have also watched as people who, at one point in their life, were following Jesus and becoming more and more like Him until one day they got distracted by the world, wandered off course, and eventually came to a place where they looked up and realized that they couldn't recognize the person they saw in the mirror. Distractions steal our time, they steal our joy, they steal our purpose, and they sometimes ruin our coffee. Friends, don't get distracted. You have a purpose that is worth pursuing and a gift worth sharing with the world. Don't get cold and gross.

I'd be willing to bet you've made a mistake or two because of distractions. I know I have. I can vividly remember a specific summer day at my grandmother's house when I was about 10 years old. She had a pool and on this particular afternoon I was in the backyard swimming. When I got bored, I got out of the pool, dried off a little, and decided I would take my rollerblades out for a spin. I loved rollerblading. I was really good at it. And I was fast. Like, really fast. In order to prove my speed, I decided I would challenge my dog, an eighty-pound rottweiler, to a race. I brought him out to the road where I was skating, said "GO!" And took off. He of course followed me but never passed me. I assumed that meant I was faster than my dog and thus, the fastest boy on the blades. Case closed. X-Games, here I come. Later that day, my dad told me that the reason I won this so called "race" was because the dog didn't understand how a race worked. He went on to say that if I really wanted to see how fast I was, I should throw the dog's ball and race him to that. At first, I thought,

"I've got nothing to prove," I mean, I had already beaten him. The best decision for me and my family at this time was to retire at the top of my game, undefeated. The GOAT of racing a dog on roller blades.

DISTRACTIONS ARE THE NUMBER ONE
KILLER OF PURPOSE.

The next day started out the same. I was in the pool, got bored, got out, put the skates on, reminded my dog that he had nothing on my speed, and together we headed for the road. It was time to come out of my incredibly short retirement for one. More. Race. It just made sense. I had a lot left in me. I'll retire when the stats drop! After racing up and down the street a few times I thought, "Why not? Let's try out this ball thing." So, I threw the ball, and I took off. I gave it everything I had. I pushed so hard with my legs it was as if I was trying to push the earth down. I pumped my arms and swayed my body back and forth with the precision that only an elite athlete possesses. I was certain I broke the sound barrier but when I looked up, I was about a quarter of the way down the street and my dog was already at the ball. I got smoked. Like, a lot. For most, this would have been a significant hit to the pride, and a major setback on what could have been a promising career in speed blading. But not for me. For me, I saw an opportunity. An opportunity to go much faster. All I needed now was his leash.

I sprinted into the house to retrieve it. I hooked the leash up to his collar, went down to the road and got out his trusty tennis ball. I drew back and threw the ball as hard as I could. Like a racer out of the gate my dog took off after the ball just like he was trained to do. The slack in the leash disappeared quickly and before I knew it, I was rolling... at dog speed. I could feel the wind in my hair and the sun on my face. I could see the houses in my periphery becoming a blurred wall of blending colors as I went faster and faster. It was amazing and even better, things were going exactly as I had planned it. Nothing could stop me now. I couldn't believe how awesome this moment was. And that's when it happened. The ball hit something in the street and bounced off to the side of the road. I followed the ball with my eyes and stopped watching my dog just long enough to miss the fact that he had taken a hard left to chase the ball into a neighboring yard. I learned quickly that while roller blades can roll at dog speed, they cannot turn at dog speed. The leash yanked my body ninety degrees to the west, but my momentum kept me going due north. This was not ideal. My feet came off the ground and for a moment, I was flying. I could see the earth beneath me, and, for a split second, it got farther away as I ascended toward the heavens. At some point mid-flight I remembered that I never put a shirt on after I got out of the pool. This was going to end badly. Unfortunately, the old adage proved true and that which goes up, must come down. And come down I did. I took the brunt of the impact across my hands, chest, and stomach. I'm sure I slid over 100 feet but who can say. All I know is that I was in a great deal of pain. I ran into the house and got into a cold shower trying to make the hurting stop but instead I felt like I had been set on fire*. In all of this, my dog was absolutely no help as all he cared about was his stupid ball. Apparently, dogs are only man's best friend if there are no tennis balls in the vicinity. Thankfully, I walked away only moderately scathed.

Many would tell me that I would have escaped that pain if I had never tried dog blading in the first place. While that may be true, I also would never have been able to travel at the speed of dog. Instead, I maintain that I would have pulled it off if I hadn't gotten distracted and kept my eyes on the dog. Had I seen him turn, I would have let go of the leash and simply coasted until my momentum dropped to a safe velocity and I regained control of my skates. Here's what I think the lesson in all of that actually is: we often experience great pain when we get caught up in distractions. Think about the drivers that crash because they get distracted by their phones, fires that start in kitchens because someone got distracted and let oil spill onto a gas burner, or the number of times we can't remember where we left our phone because we are distracted by the person we are talking to on our phone. Distractions are dangerous.

WE OFTEN EXPERIENCE GREAT PAIN WHEN WE GET CAUGHT UP IN DISTRACTIONS.

When I think of the danger of distractions, I think of the story of Samson from Judges chapters 13 through 16. Samson was a man with an enormous amount of potential. Scripture says that he was blessed by the Lord and that the Spirit of the Lord stirred within him. Before he was even born, his parents were told by an angel of the Lord that his purpose would be to rescue God's chosen people from their captors, the Philistines. He had his purpose spelled out from day negative two-hundred and eighty. He didn't have to go to a seminar, get a life coach, or take a single personality assessment to figure It out. Samson probably didn't even know his enneagram number. I imagine it to be an eight. You know, the strong, commanding, and intense type that struggle with domineering over people and fear intimacy. Samson could have been great friends with Darth Vader. Vader was also an eight. But then again, he could have been a seven. He was after all always chasing the experience of the moment with a complete disregard for any consequences. Maybe Samson and legendary pirate Captain Jack Sparrow would be a more appropriate duo. The captain was a raging seven. But let's get back to Samson. God literally told his parents, "This is what Samson's life will be all about." To me, that feels like the dream. Most days, I am confident that I am where I belong doing what I am supposed to be doing, but even still it would be nice for the Lord Himself to send me a thumbs up emoji from time to time. I mean, is that really too much to ask?

Unfortunately, clarity does not always equal effectiveness. Samson's journey would be self-inflicted setback after self-inflicted setback, each rooted in distraction. Samson's marriages – yes plural – were messy and based solely on lust and infatuation. He constantly made the wrong choice and chased the wrong things. Instead of focusing on his purpose he was distracted by his own power, pleasure, and desire. Because of this, the people of Israel remained captive to the Philistines while Samson remained captive to his own ego. Eventually, Samson's distractions would cost him the key gift God had given, his strength. With his strength gone, Samson's enemies took him captive, gouged out his eyes, and used him for entertainment purposes. Behold, the mighty Samson.

Thankfully, Samson's story didn't end there. At this point Samson, in a moment of desperation, refocuses on why he was put on this planet: to rescue his people from the hand of the Philistines. Samson prays and asks God to restore his strength so that he can get revenge on the Philistines. God answers his prayer and Samson takes down the support pillars that held up the pagan temple killing many Philistines and himself. This is not a happy ending and certainly not how God would have wanted this scene to play out. Because of distractions, Samson's purpose was reduced to an act of revenge. Samson didn't want to rescue God's people; he wanted revenge on the people who caused his blindness. Even in death, Samson was still distracted by his own desires and a selfish need for power. It was never about God, it was never about purpose or calling, it was all about Samson and his longings of the moment. OK, Samson was a total seven. Thankfully, God can use even our selfish desires for His glory and purpose. When we get distracted, even the best cup of coffee ends up cold and bitter. And like Samson, "cold and bitter" will eventually describe our lives if we let distractions derail us from our purpose.

Instead of growing cold and bitter like Samson, be like Nehemiah, a guy who refused to let distractions win the day. When we fight through the distractions and maintain focus, we usually find something amazing on the other side. Nehemiah illustrates this so well. You can find his story in the book of Nehemiah. It's named after him. That's how you know he's a real one.

Nehemiah was an Israelite exile serving as a government official in Persia. His situation was very similar to that of Daniel, Shadrach, Meshach, and Abednego but his role was a bit unique. Nehemiah was the king's royal cup bearer. The job description basically read "taste the king's food to make sure it's not poisoned and other duties as assigned." I can't imagine the fear that comes with a job like that. At least he's sampling great food from the royal table so, if each meal could be his last, at least it would be a good one. We might see this position as being just another servant, but the cupbearer was one of the most trusted positions in the king's cabinet. As cupbearer, Nehemiah literally held the king's life in his hands. Nehemiah took his position seriously and served his king well. One day Nehemiah received a message from his hometown that the wall and the gates were in ruin. Basically, the city lies defenseless, and the people are disorganized and in disgrace. Immediately Nehemiah goes to God in prayer and seeks wisdom. The next day, Nehemiah takes the king his wine and the king notices that Nehemiah is sad... for the first time ever. Did you catch that? Scripture tells us that this is literally the first time the king has ever seen Nehemiah sad and because of that the king takes notice. He asks Nehemiah why he is sad, and Nehemiah responds by telling the story of his destroyed homeland and disgraced people. The king then asks, "How can I help?" and Nehemiah makes a bold request for resources, protection, and permission to lead a renovation project. Basically, Nehemiah puts in a request for an all-expense paid leave of absence to go work on a foreign building initiative.

In what must have been a shocking moment, the king grants everything Nehemiah asks for. So, Nehemiah gets to work. He packs his camel and heads to Jerusalem where, over the next 52 days, Nehemiah and his team would completely rebuild the walls of the desolate city. It's an incredible accomplishment. But if we zoom in on the story, we see that it is riddled with potential distractions that could have been huge pitfalls. Nehemiah could have been distracted by the needs of his people or by opposition from Israel's enemies. Throughout his project, Nehemiah is ridiculed, attacked, and threatened to the point where his workers need to work with their tools in one hand and a sword in the other. And you thought you were in a hostile work environment! But Nehemiah does not waver, he does not slow down, and he does not give up. He knew that God didn't call him to Jerusalem to get involved in politics and foreign policy, He called him to build a wall. And that is what he did. Nehemiah built a wall and used that accomplishment to lead his people back into an authentic relationship with the Lord. I love the way Nehemiah responds when confronted with one of his distractions, a man named Sanballat, in Nehemiah 6:3. Just prior, Sanballat tries to convince Nehemiah to take a break and come down from the wall so that they could "just talk." Nehemiah knows they are plotting to attack him, and he says, "I am doing a great work and I cannot come down." He didn't go down, he didn't leave the wall, and he didn't walk away from his purposes because of a distraction.

There were so many things that could have distracted Nehemiah along the way, but he never succumbed. He could have been distracted by fear right at the start. Appearing sad in the presence of the king was an offense punishable by death but Nehemiah wasn't distracted by that fear and instead of covering up his sadness, he approached the king with authenticity. That authenticity is what opened the door for Nehemiah to take the next step. Once he got to that next step, he could have been distracted by the logistics and the need for resources. He was a captive in a foreign land who had no property, no rights, and no power. What he did have was influence and instead of being distracted by what he didn't have, he used the influence he had cultivated over years to secure the resources and time he needed to live out his purpose. He could have been distracted by the threats and intimidation tactics of Sanballat and the other enemies of Israel. Instead, he found ways to motivate his people and rather than slowing down, he and his people stayed focused and finished the wall in a mere 52 days. Just as getting distracted can lead to great pain, facing down our distractions and pushing through them can be the key that unlocks the door to your next step.

IF YOU ARE PURSUING YOUR PURPOSE YOU
ARE DOING A GREAT WORK

As we wrap up our journey from the seed to the cup be encouraged that if you are pursuing your purpose you, like Nehemiah, are doing a great work. Whether you are leading a ministry, running a business, managing your household, or working on a degree, if you are pursuing your purpose you are doing a great work. It doesn't matter if you are leading a team of fifty employees or an art project with one toddler, you are doing a great work. Don't get distracted. Don't give up. Don't walk away. Don't. Come. Down. And whatever you do, don't forget that cup!

This is number two on my list of things that feel the closest to being set on fire without actually being set on fire. In the context of this book, it's also a pretty solid callback – the highest form of comedy.

CHAPTER ELEVEN

YOUR LIFE IN A HILL OF BEANS

"THE ONLY IMPOSSIBLE JOURNEY IS THE ONE YOU NEVER BEGIN."

—TONY ROBBINS

People have long said that it is the ability to use tools that separate humans from animals. But my friend Travis recently reminded me that monkeys also use tools, maybe even more effectively than some humans. They use sticks to pry and dig, stones to crush and process their food, and some species of monkeys even customize these stone tools based on the job they are doing or the prey they are hunting. The ability to use tools doesn't make someone human, it simply shows that they have opposable thumbs and a basic ability to problem solve. My friend went on to say that what actually separates humans from animals is our ability to share our stories. We are the species that tell stories, that transfer knowledge from one generation to the next. It is this ability to transfer knowledge that allows us to progress as a species. The fact that we humans don't have to learn every single piece of information on our own, that we can learn from the discoveries of previous generations, allows us to draw from a collective well of knowledge and go even deeper in the pursuit of greater knowledge and wisdom. Stories allow us to connect with, relate to, and understand one another. They allow us to see a bigger picture than what the facts may show. Stories take us on a journey and leave us different than we were before. Stories allow us to celebrate the high points and sorrow in the pain of those closest to us. Stories allow us to connect with the life experiences of others and learn, grow, and develop without having to experience the pain of mistakes firsthand. Stories inspire us to become brave, disciplined, compassionate, empathetic, loving, kind, and just all around better. Stories engage our brain, activate our imaginations, and capture our hearts. If you can't experience something firsthand, the next best place to be is looking across a cup of coffee, listening to a great storyteller who has lived it.

I hope my stories have allowed you to experience new adventures, places, and situations that were previously a mystery. I hope you have been challenged in areas you may have neglected. I hope you finish this book with new courage to step up, step out, and step into the dreams and purposes that God has placed within you. I hope you've come to see

Jesus in a new way and perhaps see a little more clearly how much He loves you. And I hope my stories inspire you to share your own stories with others. You need to share your stories because they matter and are your greatest tool to help others who are experiencing the situations, hardships, or pain you have experienced. Share your gifts, your talents, and your purpose because what you have is something that the world needs. The Apostle Paul tells us this very clearly in 1 Corinthians 12. He writes that we are the body of Christ and we each have gifts, talents, and abilities that are useful for building up the entire Kingdom. He tells us that just like our physical bodies, no one part can say to another you're not needed. He says,

> The eye cannot say to the hand, "I don't need you!" And the head cannot say to the feet, "I don't need you!" On the contrary, those parts of the body that seem to be weaker are indispensable, and the parts that we think are less honorable we treat with special honor. And the parts that are unpresentable are treated with special modesty, while our presentable parts need no special treatment. But God has put the body together, giving greater honor to the parts that lacked it, so that there should be no division in the body, but that its parts should have equal concern for each other. If one part suffers, every part suffers with it; if one part is honored, every part rejoices with it. (1 Cor. 12:21-26 NIV)

This means you – yes you – matter and have a gift that is worth sharing. There is a need in the world that only you are designed to meet. There is an idea, an encouraging word, a piece of art, a melody, or a story in you that no one else can bring to the world. The part you play is critical, don't miss the opportunity to share it. I can't imagine how different history would be if Joseph didn't work with excellence while he was in captivity, if Moses didn't go back to Egypt, if Joshua hadn't spent time serving as Moses' assistant, if David had killed Saul when he had the opportunity, or if Nehemiah had been distracted and let fear stop him from approaching the king. Imagine what would be missing if Esther didn't walk into the throne room, if Daniel had bowed to the king, or if his friends worshiped that statue. And what would the history of our faith look like if Paul refused to acknowledge a real encounter with Jesus and live his life following him. Every one of these people risked everything to pursue their purpose. They faced ridicule, alienation, bodily harm and even death and yet, they went forward. They walked through pain, through suffering, and through imprisonment, but they kept taking that next step. They allowed their pain to be their story and their trials to be their classrooms, their gyms, and their crucibles. They allowed their losses to propel them forward and their setbacks became springboards. Life hurts but that pain is never meaningless.

LIFE HURTS BUT THAT PAIN IS
NEVER MEANINGLESS.

If you remember a few chapters ago, I wrote about the seven years I spent searching for my purpose after I stepped away from youth ministry. As I said, it was a long, painful, painstaking process. The most painful parts were all the times I had to say, "I guess this isn't it. Now what?" Each of those times felt like admitting to myself that I wasn't good enough. I wasn't a good enough worship leader, I wasn't a good enough video editor, I wasn't a good enough store manager. You get the point. Every "failure" felt like the end. Imagine having that conversation in your head every few months for seven years. Maybe you don't have to imagine. Maybe you've been there, or maybe you're there right now. Those seasons hurt, but they don't have to hurt for nothing. How about one more story for the road? A coffee story in a to-go cup!

My friends and family (and you, dear reader) obviously know that I love coffee. So, from time to time, I get a new or obscure coffee as a gift. I love these times. I love getting to try new things. New experiences, new foods, new places, and yes, new coffees, are always a fun time. I am not a picky eater and I really appreciate good flavor so, most of the time, I really enjoy these new things. Even in the times when a new thing is less than enjoyable, I can usually find at least something good about it. However, there are times when one of these new things just doesn't land in the way the creator intended it to land. It hits different, but not a good kind of different. Simply stated, sometimes new things are gross.

Not too long ago I received a bag of coffee as a gift from a good friend. It sounded like a good combination of flavors, and I was excited to try it. I got it ground, took it home, and brewed myself a whole pot. I poured it in my favorite mug and took that illustrious first sip. Nope. Not good. I thought, "Maybe I should take another sip. It'll be better the second time, right?" Nope. The second sip was no different. In fact, I think I liked it a little less the second time. My inner voice came back, "I should probably at least finish the cup. It's the polite thing to do and maybe it's like jazz music. You just need to keep playing the wrong note until it sounds right. It'll come around." Out of nowhere I am pretty sure I heard a narrator who sounded exactly like Morgan Freeman say, "But it did not come around."

I made it about two-thirds of the way through the cup when I decided it was time to stop torturing myself and move on. I poured it out, washed my coffee pot (like a lot), and brewed myself a new pot of my go to beans. Crisis averted. That bag of coffee sat in my cabinet forgotten for a few weeks. Finally, one day I came across it again. I realized it had gone completely stale and I finally made peace with the fact that it was time to throw it away. Those poor beans never had a chance. They never accomplished their intended purpose. I decided they weren't for me, and I pushed them aside, where they simply took up space until I finally threw them away.

Unfortunately, for some of us that sounds a lot like our lives. If we look back, we remember a point where we had a dream, a plan, a purpose. We were excited about living out that purpose and sharing our gift with the world. Then, someone told us we weren't good enough, or we weren't the right blend of skills or flavors, or that we didn't have what it takes. For some crazy reason, we believed them. We let the voice of one person or one situation completely derail us and now we simply exist taking up space at a desk or in a cubicle where we are not being utilized and not using our gifts and now our dreams are going stale. We may think no one knows or no one notices but that staleness is beginning to become obvious to people around us and eventually, we will get thrown away or tossed aside. And honestly, that may be the best thing that could happen.

Near the end of my seven-year drift I spent two years working on staff at a church in Colorado. I joined the staff as the Leadership Development pastor but was asked to serve as the interim worship pastor after the original worship pastor moved away. Once we filled that position, our leadership team and I crafted a position in which I was able to lead some of the church's creative processes. At the end of two years, the church was unfortunately not able to financially support my position and they had to let me go. I was devastated. Actually, I was angry. It felt like I was being thrown away, tossed aside. It felt like I was being told that I still didn't have what it takes to do effective ministry. That I didn't lead people well enough. That what I had to offer wasn't valuable enough to the team or the people of the community. So many thoughts filled my head. I allowed so many words and labels to attach themselves to me. Words like "worthless," "failure," "inadequate," "broken," "over," and "lacking" played on a constant loop and refused to go away. I spent sleepless nights in fear that I wouldn't be able to provide for my family and I sleepwalked through the days just trying to survive. Things got pretty dark for me and would have probably gone very differently had I not had an amazing counselor who helped me navigate this time. (Shout out to getting counseling when you need it. You're not weak for getting help, you are strong. Weakness is hiding your issues and trying to pretend you have it all together. If you need help, reach out!)

In this season, there was a huge part of me that wanted to give up, to just be done with ministry and go back to the coffee shop. But there was a larger part that screamed, "this is not the end! There is so much more in you!" Thankfully, that voice was right. It wasn't the end. Instead, it was a chance to find the place where my unique flavor fit. Think back to the weird coffee. It came in a package with an artful design and a backstory about how these flavors come together to make you feel all warm and cozy like you are inside of a Christmas sweater. You know what that suggests? Someone is buying and drinking this stuff! I don't know or understand who or why, but that gross coffee is out here bringing joy and #goodvibes to someone, somehow.

As much as it hurt, that experience became key in ending my season of drift. All of a sudden, I was forced to identify exactly what my unique flavor was and where it fit. After my counselor shook me out of my pity party, I got to work to figure out what was next. I was determined that whatever I did next was going to be in pursuit of my unique flavor. It would be the thing I could commit my life to. I refused to take that decision lightly and began doing some deep heart work to identify what that could be. I made a list of past jobs, volunteer roles, service projects, and organizations I had been involved with. Then I evaluated each of those past endeavors through the lens of joy and fruit.

I started with joy because I was in a season in which I really needed to be reminded that I have experienced incredible amounts of joy throughout my life. I asked myself through all of my past experiences, jobs, and activities, "What were the things that brought me the most joy?" This question pointed me to things like leading worship, writing, leading teams, operating an espresso bar, youth ministry, playing football, and creating art among other things. Unfortunately, given my stature and my ever so slightly less-than-elite athletic ability, pro football was off the table, so I went ahead and threw that one out. Although, you never know, it could happen, so I am still hanging on to my four years of NCAA eligibility.

The next question I began to explore was the idea of fruit. As I looked back at my life, I asked myself what jobs and experiences produced the most fruit. In other words, where did I have a track record of success or proven results? I identified areas like leadership development, recruitment, youth ministry, kid's ministry, running the coffee shop, and the Star Wars iPhone game. No joke, I was top 50 worldwide. I was kind of a big deal. Unfortunately, Star Wars mobile gaming is probably not something one should consider their life's calling so, like NFL quarterback, I removed that one from the list pretty quickly.

Finally, all I had left to do was figure out where those two lines intersected. In what areas was I both experiencing great joy and producing tangible fruit. I had a feeling that at the intersection of these two points, I would finally understand who God created me to be. For me and my life, the intersection point between joy and fruit was in pouring into the lives of kids and students. There were plenty of things I enjoyed doing that just didn't have the results. And on the other side, there were several things I am good at that just do not spark joy. When I finally realized that impacting the next generation was what resided at the intersection of joy and fruit, I felt like I had just discovered an oil well while trying to repair a sprinkler head in my backyard. It was as if all of a sudden, the world made sense and I knew what I needed to do. I was stoked and couldn't wait to share. I found my wife and, with every ounce of energy and excitement I had, exclaimed, "I need to get back into youth ministry. I have to do this. Doing this is going to be the thing that helps me thrive once again." I'll never forget her response. She said, "I know. I've been telling you that for the last seven years." Thanks babe. Always coming in hot with the truth. (In addition to counseling, I also strongly recommend listening to your spouse. Preferably seven years earlier.)

All of that is to say, if you want to find your calling, take a trip to find your joy. Inventory your life and find those moments where you couldn't think of another place you'd rather be. The moments in which time seemed to slow down and all seemed right with the world. What are the moments when you had that goofy smile on your face because you couldn't help but think of how lucky you were to be right there, right then? That's the joy part. And I promise it's in there somewhere. You may have to dig deep. Commit to the emotional excavation. It's worth it.

Once you discover that joy, it's time to look for the fruit and start stacking those wins. Find the moments in your life in which you were proud of a job well done. These are the moments in which you accomplished a big goal you never thought you would accomplish or the moments when you made a huge impact or difference in someone's life. Find the times when you heard, "We never could have done this without you," and gather them up in the "fruit" pile. These are the things you are good at or have a natural aptitude for. Run with those. You have those skills and talents for a reason. Maybe they're not all THE thing but they are all in your tool belt for a reason.

The items that find their way on to both lists are the ones you really want to explore. Those are worth pursuing. And somewhere in there I am confident that you'll find something worth committing your life to. Don't lean too heavily into the joy side at the expense of the fruit. You may end up pursuing something that is fun or attractive, but you will burn out because you're not effective. And don't go all in on fruit to the neglect of joy. You may accomplish a lot, hear a lot of praise, and even be described as successful, but in the end your joy will get choked out and slowly die. It takes both to live your purpose. It takes both joy and fruit to be your best. (See fig. a)

fig. a

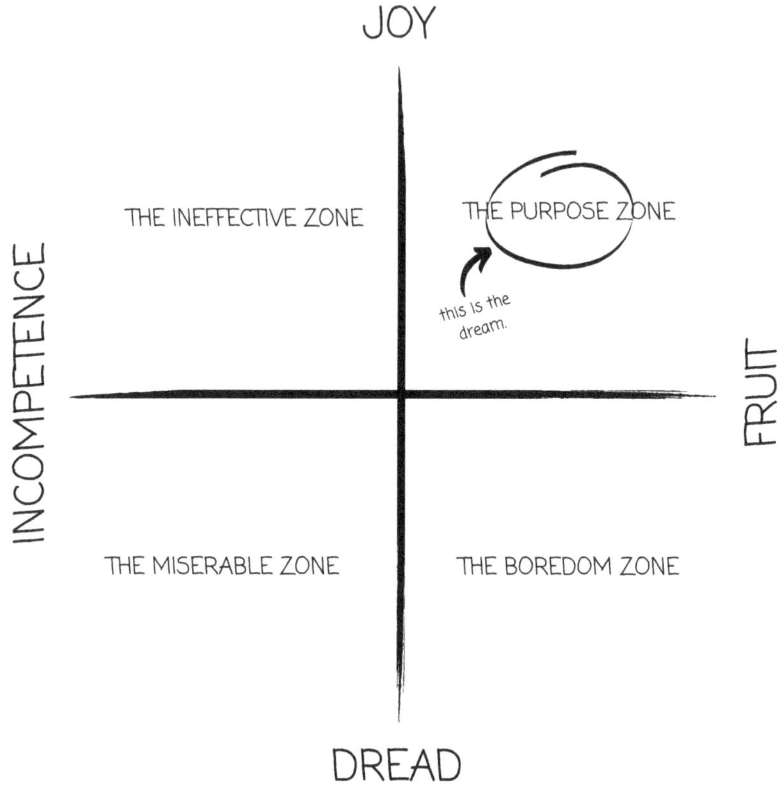

John 10:10 describes Jesus as having come to give His followers life and life to the fullest. I believe that this full life happens when joy and fruit are both present and active in our lives. Ultimately, both are gifts from Him for our benefit and for the advancement of His kingdom, but we have a part to play in tracking them down and activating them in our lives. God wants you to partner with Him to produce the unique flavor that is you.

If you haven't already, I hope you find what that flavor is. Remember, it's not about a particular job you do or role you fill. While we can, and hopefully do, find a level of fulfillment in these things, your flavor is instead all about what you uniquely bring to the world. I hope you have found a place where your flavor is appreciated because it is so needed. You have what it takes. You have a story to tell. You have a gift to share. You have a unique flavor that the world needs to experience.

This book may be over but, like the best cups of coffee, it's only the beginning. My favorite cups of coffee are always right after I wake up. I have the entire day in front of me and that fresh cup helps me to kick it off with a burst of energy that will propel me forward. Let this be that burst of energy for you. Maybe you are reading this book closer to the beginning of your journey. You are just starting out in your career and you have your whole life in front of you. Explore joy and fruit now and let what you discover guide you as you start down this path.

FULL LIFE HAPPENS WHEN JOY AND FRUIT ARE
BOTH PRESENT AND ACTIVE IN OUR LIVES.

But maybe you're reading this book closer to the middle. The middle of any journey can be the most difficult part. The middle usually lacks the excitement that was present at the beginning. At the beginning, we get to think and dream. We get to look at a blank slate with nothing but opportunity before us. At the beginning, others are excited for us and they're cheering us on. But in the middle, the cheers fade and we can find ourselves alone. But there is another great truth about coffee that has sadly been overlooked up to this point: it's just as good in the middle of the day. When the afternoon lull is in full force, a good cup of coffee can be just what the doctor ordered.

If you're in the middle of your journey and you feel like your energy is waning, maybe it's time to explore the joy and fruit of your life again. Allow this time to be the mid-journey pick me up that helps you get back on track. As they say, the best time to plant a tree was twenty years ago, but the second-best time is right now. I say, the best cups of coffee are first thing in the morning but the second-best cups are in the early afternoon! Maybe you're in the afternoon of your life, it's not too late to change course. Remember, Vera Wang entered the fashion industry at forty, Samuel L. Jackson got his first major film role at forty-three, Julia Child wrote her first cookbook at fifty, and Grandma Moses (one of the most prolific painters in modern history) began painting at seventy-eight years old. She eventually sold one of her paintings for 1.2 million dollars! It's never too late to start chasing your dreams and pursuing your purpose. All you have to do is clear the fields and start planting. Seriously, put the coffee down and get to it! I can't wait to see what happens next!

ACKNOWLEDGEMENTS

THANKS A LATTE

TO MY WIFE, WHO SLEPT THROUGH MOST OF THE TIME I SPENT ON THIS PROJECT Thank you for telling me this message was within me. Thank you for the hours you put into making this book look awesome, Thank you for the support you have given me from day one. Thank you for the sacrifices you have made to allow me to follow my dreams, goals, and passions. None of what you have given has gone unnoticed. Without you, I wouldn't be who I am today.

TO MY GIRLS You make my life fun. You never cease to amaze me or make me laugh. I love watching you chase your dreams, I love watching you grow, and I love being your dad.

TO MY DAD We've been on a crazy journey that's been filled with ups, downs, and everything in between. Thank you for never giving up on me or our relationship. Thanks for having the strength to admit weaknesses and for refusing to quit inviting me on that hike, that hike that changed everything. I hope we get to tell our story some day. Its one of the best stories I've ever heard. There are a lot of my stories in this book, but that one is one of the best!

TO MY AMAZING IN-LAWS You've always challenged me to keep moving forward, encouraged me when I've wanted to quit, and supported me in every crazy idea and adventure I can come up with. Thank you for believing in me in every season, especially the ones in which I didn't believe in myself.

TO GRAM Thank you for helping me make this dream come true and for supporting me through many phases of life. You've shared so many great stories that have taught me more than you know. I'm still fascinated by mums and how they get their color. Thanks for that one and so many more!

TO CHRIS AND MORGAHN Thanks for being a constant source of encouragement, for telling me to finish this book, and for the countless prayers and conversations while we contemplate life and faith over wings or mexican food. Thanks for helping me make this dream come true.

TO JON ACUFF AND THE GUARANTEED GOALS COMMUNITY A lot of people told me I should write this book, but it was you who showed me I could. Without your support, encouragement, and accountability, this book would have remained one more item on a long list of unaccomplished goals. Thank you for the push and the reminder that all it takes is a goal!

TO MY MOM, MY SISTER, AND THE REST OF MY FAMILY, EXTENDED FAMILY, AND FRIENDS WHO HAVE BECOME FAMILY You've all been a source of inspiration and amazing stories. Thank you for being part of the moments in which God has whispered to me. Thanks for being a tangible representation of what Jesus is like. And thank you for being His voice in times when I couldn't hear Him for myself.

TO EVERYONE WHO HAS MADE MY LIFE A LITTLE MORE MAGICAL, ENCOURAGED ME TO KEEP GOING, AND SPOKEN LIFE OVER ME, MY FAMILY, AND MY DREAMS Thank you for being part of my journey in every season from planting to that magical first sip and everything in between. I couldn't have done this without you.

AND TO YOU DEAR READER Thank you for taking a chance on a new author and joining me on this journey. Here's to the next step, the next phase, or the next season. Tell awesome stories and make some magic happen!

ABOUT

Brandon is a pastor, author, and speaker who loves to help people understand a little more about Jesus, their purpose, and personal values. Brandon has been married to his wife, Ashley, since 2008 and they have two daughters. Brandon and his family are from Charleston, South Carolina but have lived in Colorado, Nebraska, and now, North Carolina. Brandon serves on his church staff and loves speaking at churches, camps, conferences, and anywhere else that he can help those in attendance take a step forward in their faith, life, or career. He has seen first-hand the positive impact that defining personal values and a clear purpose statement can have, and wants to help as many people as possible experience those same benefits. Brandon has worked in many industries including customer service, retail, food and beverage, and ministry, and knows that every industry and every individual thrives when people are being valued and are working from a place of purpose.

OTHER WORKS

THIS AWESOME LIFE

This Awesome Life is a collection of stories that point to purpose.

BLOG: thisawesome.life
PODCAST: brandonhair.me/podcast

FINDING YOU: DISCOVER YOUR PERSONAL VALUES AND LIFE MISSION

Finding You is a powerful tool that helps you live out your God-given purpose by equipping you to identify what matters most and pursue those things. It empowers you with the tools needed to say no to the things that don't align with your values allowing you the space to say yes to the things that do. Finding You is a practical tool that will give you a step-by-step guide to creating a filter for every decision that comes your way. Live your life on purpose by identifying your values and living them out. *Available on Amazon*

FIND BRANDON ON SOCIAL MEDIA

Instagram.com/brandonhair

Facebook.com/authorbrandonhair

Youtube.com/@brandonlhair

BRANDONHAIR.ME